YACHTING IN THE
NORTHERN
MEDITERRANEAN

AA

YACHTING IN THE
NORTHERN MEDITERRANEAN

Text by

Roberto Franzoni

Franco Masiero

Carla Notarbartolo di Sciara

Paola Pozzolini

Martino Spadari

AA

Translated by Valerie Palmer

Photographs by:

Carlo Borlenghi, pp. 30-31, 42-43, 62-63, 103, 105, 106-107, 107,
110-111, 126-127, 129, 131, 200-201; *East Coast,* p. 22; *Focus Team,*
pp. 39, 44-45, 46-47, 48, 49 (above), 52-53, 55, 64-65, 71, 72-73, 75,
80-81, 86, 88-89, 93, 94-95, 98 (below), 100-101, 108, 108-109, 112,
113, 114-115, 118, 119, 120-121, 122-123, 123, 124, 132-133, 134-135,
139, 141, 142-143, 148-149, 150, 152-153, 156, 157, 160, 161, 162-163,
164-165, 173, 174, 178-179, 180-181, 182, 183, 184, 185, 186-187, 188,
189, 190-191, 194, 195, 196, 197, 203; *Roberto Franzoni,* pp. 69, 78-79,
81, 82-83, 87, 90-91, 91, 92-93, 98 (above), 136-137; *Alessandro Gui,*
p. 13; *Paola Lovato,* pp. 49 (below), 67; *Albano Marcarini,* pp. 146,
151, 168-169; *Franco Masiero,* pp. 14, 15, 21, 24, 25, 26, 28, 29, 31,
32-33, 34, 35, 36, 37, 56; *Overseas,* p. 54; *Laura Ronchi,* pp. 176-177;
Zefa, pp. 58-59, 144-145, 147, 154-155, 158-159, 166-167, 171, 193,
198-199, 202

Distributed in the United Kingdom by the Publishing Division of The Automobile Association,
Fanum House, Basingstoke, Hampshire RG21 2EA.

This edition published 1990 by The Automobile Association,
Fanum House, Basingstoke, Hampshire RG21 2EA.

A CIP catalogue record for this book is available from the British
Library.

ISBN 0 7495 0037 9

Printed and bound in Italy by Arnoldo Mondadori Editore, Verona

CONTENTS

INTRODUCTION

The Mediterranean is the most famous sea in the world. Its exceptionally mild climate, unique vegetation and millennia of history, combined with its strategic position as a pivotal point between east and west, have spread its fame all over the world. Compared with the oceans and other seas on Earth, it is of fairly recent formation, although it has undergone all manner of changes in the process: it has filled and emptied eighteen times; it has been both a lake and a desert; it has shrunk and expanded. More recently, however, from a historical point of view, it has played a leading role in European civilization with the culture of the Western world having grown up and flourished along its shores. A sea surrounded by land – as its name implies – covering over 2.5 million km^2 (1 million sq. miles), its maximum length from east to west is 3,700 km (2,300 miles), and from north to south, 700 km (435 miles).

From the sixteenth century B.C., people living along its shores engaged in both profitable trade and violent conflict, the Mediterranean forming the only effective means of communication between lands which lay a great distance apart. In the period before Christ, Cretans, Mycenaeans, Phoenicians and Romans used its waters – occasionally treacherous, but more often calm, and without currents, tides or whirlpools – interweaving the distinctive strands of their varied cultures along its shores. From the Middle Ages the sea routes became increasingly busy as first the Saracens and then the Venetian Republic and the Ottoman Empire established their power in a succession of great sea voyages, epic battles and flourishing trade, in their aim to dominate ever greater areas of sea and land. From the sixteenth to the eighteenth century,

the alternation of commerce and war in the waters of the Mediterranean saw the Aragonese pitted against the French. The English, armed with less than peaceful motives, entered the foray in the Mediterranean via the Strait of Gibraltar.

The Mediterranean is divided into two halves – the eastern Mediterranean and western Mediterranean – separated by Cap Bon peninsula in Tunisia and Sicily, which are about 70 miles apart. Within the western section are the Sea of Alboran, that of the Balearics, of Corsica and Sardinia, the Ligurian and the Tyrrhenian. To the east, are the Ionian, the Adriatic, the Aegean, the Libyan Sea and the Sea of Sirte. All these place-names, apart from being a useful means of identifying the different areas, reflect a variety of local cultures, customs, traditional types of vessel and fishing methods. They also indicate different microclimates within the vast and favourable Mediterranean climatic system. This is a sea used for sport as much as for transportation, because of the wonderful prevailing meteorological conditions and ease of navigation, and the innumerable attractive locations to be found along its shores. On the threshold of the twenty-first century, *Mare Nostrum* (our sea) is host to an imposing fleet of cruisers which, if unimpressive in terms of tonnage, is certainly the largest in the world in terms of numbers. Flags from all over Europe, the Americas, the Near East and the southern hemisphere converge in the salt waters of the Mediterranean in search of beautiful scenery, and historical, ethnic and gastronomic treasures. In no other part of the world are such diverse features concentrated into such a comparatively small area, all accessible within just a few hours' sailing.

The gentle climate has progressively allowed the sailing season to be extended from April to November. Sailing in the Mediterranean is easy, exciting, and a source of endless enjoyment. The almost non-existent tides and the very weak, virtually negligible constant currents, its great depth (except in the Adriatic), the way in which the coast is broken up to provide an infinity of shelters even in cross-winds, and the numerous harbours, both ancient sea-ports and modern purpose-built marinas, make sailing holidays a possibility even for the novice sailor. The Mediterranean boasts a wide variety of coastlines with a rich assortment of architecture along its shores. The varying hues of its waters and depths, and the luxuriant vegetation often wafting heady fragrances up to the approaching vessels (particularly around Corsica and Sardinia) are all part of its immense attraction. The colours, sometimes softened by a veil of mist, sometimes sparkling, swept clean by the wind, as in the Greek islands, and the ever-changing, distinctive light found at the different latitudes within the waters of the Mediterranean (about 10° from 32 to 42 north) never fail to make a deep impression on even the most hardened and experienced of sailors. The complex historical stratification of the Mediterranean's settlements, the intricate multiracial composition of the people living along its shores and the rich artistic, archaeological and monumental heritage scattered almost carelessly along its coasts offer an infinite choice of possibilities for a Mediterranean cruise.

This guide suggests six classic Mediterranean cruise itineraries, spanning the area from east to west, and planned to make the most of the beautiful scenery along the route and the clearness of the water in those stretches. The problem of pollution is unfortunately becoming more and more evident, with dramatic consequences in some areas. It is particularly serious in an enclosed sea with a limited exchange of water into which numerous rivers discharge industrial effluent. The situation has alarmed all those who use the Mediterranean, especially the authorities of the countries along its shores who realize that urgent action is required to combat this threat. Our itineraries also take into account the availability and number of well-equipped harbours – both those of historical interest and purpose-built marinas – where one can easily replenish food, water and fuel supplies. The routes are marked with coves and inlets, and anchorages for use in the event of bad weather, or more enjoyably, in which to bathe or spend a peaceful night.

As this guide is not a pilot book, but an initial aid to planning and organizing a cruise, it does not include information on sea depths, dangers to shipping, rules or restrictions governing navigation in the waters of each country.

Charts of the Mediterranean are published by the British Admiralty. They cover the whole of the Mediterranean in sections. Relevant charts for the different itineraries in this book have been listed in the cartography section of each chapter. Similar charts are published by the equivalent hydrographic services in France (Service Hydrographique et Océanographique de la Marine – S.H.O.M.) and in Italy (Istituto Idrografico della Marina Italiana) in their respective languages.

There are also numerous publications similar to pilot books, but specifically for users of pleasure craft. Imray Laurie Norie & Wilson publish a series of Water Pilots covering different sections of the Mediterranean. Reed's Mediterranean Navigator, which is updated annually, is an extremely useful handbook. It contains a wealth of information regarding harbour regulations, how to enter them, what amenities are available and describes navigational aids as well as many other practical details.

As both the official works and those produced by private publishers run to many volumes, the most practical thing to do, having chosen an area of interest, is to acquaint yourself with the characteristics, dangers and difficulties of the area in question by studying a couple of volumes in depth. It is essential to keep these on board for consultation, even if sailing in the Mediterranean is relatively easy, and you have studied the route extensively beforehand. The emphasis in this guide book is on the charm and fascination of the areas suggested for the cruises, particularly the landscape and cultural characteristics which are obviously neglected by the official and unofficial pilot books. One such element covered is gastronomy, an extremely enjoyable aspect of the culture of a country and its people. The Mediterranean countries are particularly well supplied with natural foods and flavoursome ingredients. Once again, the trade carried on between its peoples since antiquity has helped mix recipes and traditions to such an extent that one can identify a common denominator in the Mediterranean diet: a light and nutritious diet characterized by the prevalance of vegetables, dressed with olive oil. Like wine, oil is found throughout the Mediterranean, produced by a variety of methods with such a wealth of flavours that one never tires of them. A beverage common to many parts of the Mediterranean is aniseed, a deliciously refreshing drink, which, from the French Pastis to the Italian Sambuca, Greek Ouzo and Turkish Raki reflects once more the unifying strand along the shores of this small but mighty sea.

Each itinerary in the guide has been given a chapter to itself. The various stages of the trip are outlined, and the distances are shown in nautical miles (1nm = 1,852 m or 6,080 ft). The main attractions along the route are pointed out, together with any diversions by sea or excursions on land to places of special interest. There is a feature on the local cuisine and notes on customs and folklore. Each chapter is accompanied by a concise map of the route and a short bibliography, with a list of essential maps chosen from among the best available from the various hydrographic services. Journey times have not been calculated, given the variable weather conditions in such relatively large areas, plus the fact that the trips could be undertaken by either sailing or motorboats, obviously with very different capabilities. The port of departure was chosen in some cases for

ease of access to the country in question, e.g. Athens for Greece or Marmaris for Turkey, both of which have airports. Others, like Porto Cervo for Sardinia and St. Florent for Corsica were chosen for the convenience and high standard of the port. Access was not considered a problem, given the great number of possible ways of arriving there. In the case of St Tropez on the French coast and Lošinj on the Yugoslav one, the choice of port was determined by a desire to concentrate on the areas considered most interesting.

What is the best time of year to organize a cruise in the Mediterranean? Summer automatically springs to mind with warmer air and sea temperatures and more stable weather conditions, but unfortunately this is also the busiest season. The winds are particularly gentle in the western Mediterranean in summer, except for squalls in August affecting the Gulf of Lions and Corsican and Sardinian seas in particular, where the mistral (northwest wind) can blow very strongly. This is not a good time for sailing vessels, which will be forced to use their engines for hours on end. Conversely, in the eastern Mediterranean, and the Aegean in particular, the months of July and August are the times when the meltemi is at its strongest. This is a wind which blows from the north-west to north-east and strikes the Cyclades in particular with a strength of up to force 8. It is a regular daily wind which gets up in the morning, reaches its maximum intensity in the afternoon, and dies down at night. Travelling under sail in such conditions is exciting, but hard work. Travelling by motorboat is difficult and tiring. It is not usually very windy in the Adriatic in high summer, so it is better to visit the islands of Dalmatia by motorboat at this time. However, even if the bora (from north to north-east) were to start blowing strongly, or the sirocco (from the south-east), which is not as strong, the narrowness of the straits and proximity of the islands would prevent dangerous waves from forming. The best months for all the areas are June and September. The meltemi does not blow in the Aegean at this time, and in the other areas the pattern of the wind, though variable, is stronger and more pleasant. Furthermore, in June, the daylight hours are the longest in the year, reaching an average of sixteen, allowing one to sail until evening without worrying about sailing in the dark. In September there are about twelve hours of daylight, but the mild climate and beautiful colours more than compensate for the shorter days. It is very important to keep abreast of changes in the weather at all seasons, making enquiries at the harbour office before setting out and listening to the shipping forecasts on the national radio and telecommunications services on the VHF waveband.

If you do not have a boat of your own, or do but cannot afford the time and money to transfer it to a different area, you can hire one, with or without a crew, in all the places chosen for the itineraries in this book. There has been an enormous increase in the number of vessels available for charter in the Mediterranean in recent years, particularly in the areas considered here, and plenty of different types of boat are on offer. At present the greatest demand is for yachts without crews. Boats with crews tend to be larger and much more comfortable because of the extra space and the advantage of a professional crew, but are of course much more expensive to hire. Equal

numbers of sailing and motorboats are available for hire. In any case, the boats available for charter nowadays are very modern, on average no more than three years old, and increasingly managed by large enterprises rather than small companies. One such organization is Kavos-Moorings, which administers a fleet of more than 500 vessels worldwide, half of which are distributed in the most popular parts of the Mediterranean, such as Greece and Turkey, Yugoslavia and France. The boats without crews vary from 8 to 15 m (25–50 ft) in length and can accommodate up to ten people. The cost per day, subdivided by the number of occupants, is comparable to that of a good average hotel, excluding meals, the cost of fuel and water and harbour expenses.

In the case of boats without crews, most charter companies expect you to return the vessel to the port of departure, although it is possible to leave it elsewhere by paying a supplement for a crew to bring it back and the extra days involved. Obviously these problems do not arise when hiring a boat with a crew, and you can arrange from the outset to embark at one port and disembark at another. All large towns have charter agencies which provide information and can suggest the best type of boat to suit your requirements.

DALMATIA

Lošinj–Susak–Ilovik–Brgulje–Zadar–Kornati–Šibenik–
Trogir–Hvar–Korčula–Dubrovnik–Kotor

This is a beautiful stretch of sea where the sailor will always be tempted to linger rather than just travel through. It is like an archipelago, almost a sea in its own right, full of surprises, sudden transformations, breathtaking scenery and historical and human elements that provide an endless source of interest. One could spend a lifetime exploring this coast without ever exhausting the journey possibilities. The Yugoslav coastline is about 600 km (373 miles) long as the crow flies. However, if one were to trace round all the coastlines to include every inlet and island, the figure would be 6,200 km (3,852 miles) between the mainland shore and the 725 islands; of the latter, 65 are inhabited, while the majority, about 500, are little larger than rocks.

From Lošinj to Kotor

A short stop at Lošinj, just long enough to deal with the formalities of entering Yugoslavia and to replenish food, water and fuel supplies in this well-equipped port, then off immediately in search of the first of a long series of surprises: Susak, a rocky outcrop rising from the sea and completely covered in a layer of sand. The little harbour, a tiny village inhabited by people dressed in curious costume, and the overall atmosphere, are enough to make you feel you are truly off the beaten track. Travelling on south you will reach the sheltered bay of Ilovik. Anchoring in a broad channel between the little islands of Ilovik and Sveti Petar, the only sounds are the gentle lapping of the water and the song of the cicada. Here we leave the open sea for a long stretch to negotiate an intricate network of channels and inland sea where sailing, although quite hard work

The little island of Melita, whose eleventh-century Benedictine monastery has recently been turned into a hotel, is situated in one of the two lakes at the interior of the large island of Mljet. Connected to the sea by a strait, these lakes are immersed in a landscape dominated by huge forests of oak and pine.

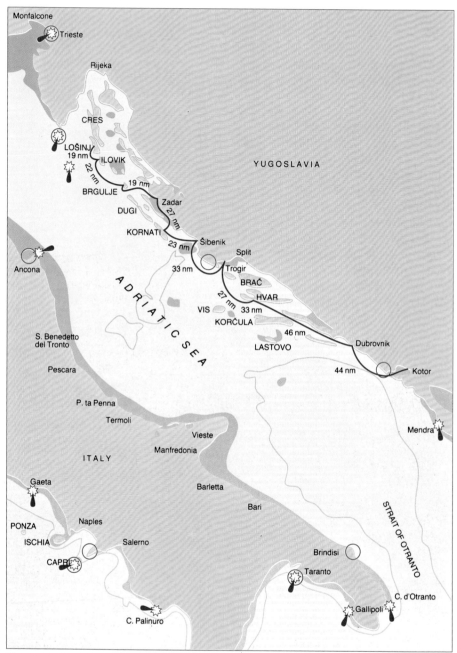

Distance covered: 293 nm.
Average temperatures: January −0.7–3.2 °C (32–38°F); July 20.2–24.7°C (68–76°F).
Prevailing winds: Bora, from the north and north-east, of varying intensity; sirocco, from the south-east, of variable intensity; mistral, from the north-west, usually a breeze.
Cartography: British Admiralty: 204 (Porto Corsini and Otok Premuda to Porto di Trieste); 220 (S. Benedetto del Tronto and Otok Vis to Porto Corsini and Otok Premuda); 200 (Vieste and Otok Lastovo to Porto Recanati and Drvenik Mali); 196 (Ulcinj to Split).
Bibliography: Blue Guide to Yugoslavia (A. & C. Black, London. W. W. Norton, New York). Adriatic Pilot – the Yugoslavian coast (Imray Laurie Norie & Wilson).

in places, will enable us to make the most of the wind without the waves ever becoming excessive. We have entered a huge archipelago of living sea, with land rising out of the water in complex shapes, its surfaces varying dramatically from a thick blanket of vegetation to bare rock and an almost lunar-like landscape. The broad channel that opens between the islands of Silba and Premuda is practically an internal sea lapping the shores of Ist and Molat. Then, passing through the Sedmovrace, one enters the unforgettable bay of Brgulje. It is something of a sacrifice to have to neglect the interior of the Kvarner Gulf with the large islands of Cres, Krk, Rab and Pag, but as we are heading south on this voyage we must gain in latitude and leave the exploration of these internal waters, for centuries the home of the Uskok pirates, for another occasion.

At Zadar we stop to visit the first of the lovely historical towns on our itinerary. The coast behind it

The Kornati archipelago is made up of more than a hundred islands: barren places, with very few houses and no running water. But the sea is beautiful here.

Opposite: the great bastion of Fort Bokar forms part of the walls that completely surround Dubrovnik, once part of the Venetian Republic: a mighty perimeter 1,940 m (1.2 miles) long, which defended the "Serenissima" republic for nearly 1,000 years.

The façade of the quaint little Romanesque church next to St Mark's Cathedral in Korčula. It faces on to the churchyard, forming a peaceful and secluded corner.

is part of the Slavonic world, and farther on lie the Levant and, beyond that, the Orient. In front of us, just before the horizon meets the sea, are the long islands of Ugljan, Pašman, Dugi Otok and many other minor ones. There is also the Kornati archipelago, composed of nearly 50 completely barren and almost indescribably beautiful islets, without water or sign of human invasion, rich only in total silence and irresistible fascination. Another broad stretch, with numerous land masses rising from the water, leads to Šibenik: we sail past an imposing fortress, enter a narrow channel into a long internal harbour surrounded by one of the towns richest in architecture and history. We could go farther in, towards Lake Prokljan, to see the Krka falls. Just south of Šibenik, at Cape Ploča, the first archipelago of Dalmatia ends and the open sea reaches the mainland. Lower down another succession of islands begins, increasingly large this time and farther apart, between channels so broad that the islands appear far away on the horizon. Trogir, aristocratic, well-preserved and peaceful, leads into this second archipelago. Then come the islands of Šolta, Brač, Vis and Hvar. The latter is worth stopping at, if only because the vaguely Venetian atmosphere that has accompanied us so far ends here. Further on, down towards Korčula, we discover the smallest and perhaps most attractive town of all: a clutch of houses built around a tiny hill. It is impressively well-preserved, silent and welcoming. We sail through the channel between the very long islands of Pelješac and Mljet, then out into the open sea until we reach Dubrovnik.

It is unbelievable that the beauty of Korčula could be surpassed, but there is even better to come in Dubrovnik, whose massive, light-coloured walls, visible on the horizon, enclose a city of illustrious traditions. For many centuries it was an independent republic, with ambassadors throughout Europe. Merchants and explorers brought it wealth, similar in many ways to the fate of the larger, more fortunate and more ambitious Venice. The archipelagos of Yugoslavia, and her internal seas, end here. As each day passes, sailing further south, one searches the sky for signs of that deep blue so characteristic of the south and, on land, other vividly typical signs of the Levant. The transition happens gradually, at the slow pace typical of boats. Still farther south, then,

SUPPLIES

There are no problems with water in the north, but the further south you travel, the more likely you are to encounter difficulties – except, of course, in the little harbours equipped for pleasure craft. Resorts will generally have big shops like supermarkets or small stores stocking just a few items. Wherever you go it is generally possible to purchase canned foods which, failing more elaborate preparations, will be sufficient to tide you over in an emergency. Meat is very good, although it is not always possible to get good cuts; sometimes distribution is a problem and you may have to make do with what is left for a day or two. Though the bread is good (doughy but with good keeping qualities), it tends to lack variety. Dalmatian cured ham is excellent; vegetables and fruit are quite good but often limited in choice. Well-known products may be purchased in the many duty-free shops but, as is often the case with such places, it is advisable to check each time whether the prices really are advantageous.

One final comment. First-time visitors may get the impression that both the shops and restaurants look a bit run-down, offering limited choice. But if you try to understand the country's situation and respect its complex historical background you will learn to feel differently about it, appreciating its unique atmosphere and valuing the widespread courtesy and gentle hospitality of its people.

into the huge fjord of the Gulf of Kotor: about 15 miles between cliff walls in a long inlet bordered by mountains nearly 2,000 m (6,500 ft) high until one reaches Kotor. There the journey ends, in a land that is almost a frontier between the western world and that of Islam.

From Lošinj to Ilovik   19 nm

We have left the long stretch of sea spanning the Kvarner Gulf behind us, a difficult undertaking if the weather is not too good. Then, as we sail off the island of Unije, the heights of Lošinj become visible. It is always an exhilarating experience to enter the long bay leading to the picturesque town of Mali Lošinj. This is also a good place to deal with the formalities of entering Yugoslavia.

This tourist port is very well equipped and the only problem is the perpetually choppy water caused by the heavy boat traffic. However, it is better to stay here at a mooring rather than choosing the quay that encloses the bay, where north winds tend to buffet and can cause serious damage. The best plan, however, is to turn towards the open sea and the island of Susak, which is directly opposite (8 nm).

This island consists of a rocky base covered in a layer composed entirely of sand and, on top of this, there are huge terraces with vines, fruit and vegetables. At the highest point, 96 m (315 ft) stands a lighthouse which emits a powerful beam visible for 25 miles, for the rather curious period of 30 seconds. The little harbour is narrow, and it is advisable to enter it only when the weather is fairly good. It is also important to note that at least half of the harbour basin is only deep enough for dinghies. You disembark on to a flat, dusty area with only a large, low building in view. To the left, however, is a large bay opening on to the sea, but less than 1 m (3 ft) deep. It is ideal for windsurfing, or just shallow bathing.

The old town is farther up, about twenty minutes' walk away, with an elderly population of a somewhat unusual appearance: stockily built, the local women wear traditional costume characterized by a short pleated skirt. There is an atmosphere of poverty and neglect: water is only available in tanks. There are a few modest restaurants and a little supermarket.

Yet this is a magical island where one can really

feel far away from the everyday world. It is worth stopping here, going along the narrow cliff face that surrounds the entire island and spending a few days there in brilliant sunshine, surrounded by crystal-clear water, soaking up the sun without seeing a living soul.

Away from Susak, the route south touches Lošinj and leads to Ilovik (11 nm), or rather to a broad channel between the islets of Ilovik and Sveti Petar. This is a first-rate anchorage, well sheltered from the sirocco (SE) and from the bora (NE). As it can accommodate numerous boats, many are usually moored there.

It is worth going this way, because it means another day spent without having to set foot on land. You can feast your eyes on the sea, enjoy all the sunlight and breezes of Dalmatia and gradually prepare for the journey into the archipelago. Myriad

Overleaf: the picturesque little town of Mali Lošinj is situated at the southern end of a long, narrow bay which is much used by pleasure craft.

View of the port of Dubrovnik (formerly Ragusa) in southern Dalmatia, the penultimate stage of our journey. Dubrovnik was the seat of a semi-independent republic from 1205 to 1208 (the Republic of Ragusa).

SLAVONIC COOKERY

The food in the Levant is characterized by strong, sometimes rather heavy flavours, intensely perfumed with aromatic herbs and every degree of sweetness up to the cloying taste of honey. All along the coast and on the more frequented islands it is quite easy to find restaurants serving very good fish and meat. It is worth being adventurous and trying any dishes recommended. Prices are perhaps a bit higher than one would expect, but never excessive. However, there is also a very economical way of eating genuine Yugoslav food. Go into one of the numerous taverns that serve simple dishes, consisting almost entirely of onion, tomato, ražnijci (kebabs), čevapčici (minced meat kebabs, see below) and pljeskavica (a kind of hamburger). It costs very little to eat in these places, the service is no more than adequate, but it is a pleasant way of feeling a little less like a tourist. The pastry shops and ice-cream parlours are all very uniform, both in terms of their ambience and the produce they sell. Try them: liking them or not is a matter of personal preference. Drinks are excellent. The national beer, with a strong flavour of malt, is very good. There is a wide choice of wines ranging from table wines to really fine wines. Žilavka (a dry white) is very well known, as is Istrian Malvasia (nearly always dry and sometimes excellent). Then there are reds like Kastelet, Merlot and Postup to name but a few. As far as spirits are concerned, choose between Maraschino (distilled from marasca cherries), Slivovitz (made from prunes) and Travarica, a kind of schnapps flavoured with herbs.

fragrances, the song of the cicada and glimpses of age-old rocks or ruins accompany us. On the shores of Sveti Petar, some large bollards remind us that the galleys which used to leave Venice bound for the Levant once moored here. We are in fact retracing those ancient and captivating routes.

From Ilovik to Zadar   41 nm

The sea has crept in between the islands but the stretches of water are still formidable: to starboard is Premuda and to port, Silba, but there is plenty of room for some satisfying sailing towards Brgulje (22 nm). You will pass high, rugged and tortuous islets, the Pettini, to arrive at Ist. The bay of Ist village provides good shelter and the surrounding countryside is pretty. Ist-Kosiraca is also worth a visit. On this itinerary, however, we continue to-wards the narrow passage between Ist and the long island of Molat. The Zapuntel channel is fine in good weather, otherwise you will need to sail right round the island up to the very broad Sedmovrace channel. To the north-west, on the island of Molat, the huge bay of Brgulje opens out. There is little to see there, just a bay with a small island at the center, one half of which is barren, and the other half overgrown with masses of wild sage. Its intense perfume is one of nature's gifts. There is even a chance of seeing a school of dolphins fishing, or simply swimming and playing. The slopes of Molat are a rich green. On the shore is a little jetty with one or two houses, including a bakery filling the air with the delightful aroma of fresh bread. For those who want a village to explore, there is a quiet and uncrowded one a short climb away. It is peaceful and timeless here, the sunset lighting up the sky in heavenly hues. Sailing is never too dangerous here, even in bad weather.

The next stretch (19 nm) leads to Zadar, and many impressive islands: leaving Dugi Otok, Zverinac, Sestrunj, Rivanj and Ugljan behind us to our right, we are already in sight of the Pašman channel. From the tourist port it is not far to the old town which is studded with many interesting architectural features, and well worth a visit. First Illyrian, then Roman, then Byzantine, Hungarian and Venetian, it was chosen by the Venetian Republic as a powerful bas-tion against the marauding Turks. It has retained its basic Roman town plan, and monuments typical of

Detail of one of the statues that adorn the church of St Chrysogonus in Zadar. There are many outstanding examples of sculpture in Dalmatia.

A.C.Y. TOURIST PORTS

In the last few years, the Adriatic Club Yugoslavia has built 16 marinas which can accommodate a total of about 5,000 pleasure boats. The facilities are excellent. The standard of facilities may not be luxurious, but the A.C.Y. marinas can more than satisfy all basic requirements.

The marinas are at Umag, Rovinij, Pula and Pomer on Istria; Supertarska Drag and Rab on the island of Rab; Žut, Piškera and Jezera on the Kornati islands; further south, Vodice, Skradin, Trogir, Split, Milna (illustrated), Vrboska and Pelmežana. Five more are under construction: one on the Brijuni islands, then at Opatija, Ilovik, Korčula and Dubrovnik.

Nautical services offered are: reception; water and electricity supply; fuel supplies; workshop for repairs and spare parts; 10-ton crane; slipway; haulage; launching; housing; fire surveillance; VHF reception; telex and telephone. Other services include: restaurants and shops; duty-free shop; car-parking; frontier post; post office; currency exchange; boutique; launderette; sports and occasionally windsurfing, sailing and deep-sea diving courses.

Moorings: keeping in mind that it is crowded in summer, one can book a long time in advance by telephone or telex, or get in touch by VHF radio shortly beforehand to find out what is available. Membership of the A.C.Y. is obtained through the purchase of an ADRIATIC PASS, and members are given a booklet of vouchers (mooring, visitors' tax, free water and electricity) for 14, 21 or 28 days, plus 2, 4 or 6 days' free mooring respectively, at any one of the 16 marinas. Besides mooring charges calculated on a daily basis at quite reasonable prices, there are rather more economical schemes for those wishing to leave the boat either in the water or on land for months, or even all year round.

what is commonly known as "Venetian" architecture have been added. It also has many characteristics that are entirely original and the Byzantine church of St Donatus is one of the finest in the whole of Dalmatia. The streets are bathed in a brilliant white light and, despite new building after the ravages of the last war, still evoke an atmosphere of an illustrious past. One can also feel the present, which is essentially Yugoslavian but also with something of an Italian feel, Italy having strong historical links with Zadar.

From Zadar to Šibenik   50 nm

Sailing through the Pašman channel, the charming little town of Biograd glides past us on our left, and from offshore we can see the busy resort of Pakoštane. Heading south-west towards the open sea, the stunning islands of the Kornati archipelago loom up on the horizon. The main one (27 nm), Kornat, is long and thin. Its seaward side is fringed with rocky outcrops forming a little world of their own, where the sea has become both a deep blue mantle and a desert of rocks. There is utter silence here, and an enchanted, almost disquieting atmosphere dominated by the power of nature. There are those who, having sailed all round the world, return here year after year, repeating the same cruise. One never tires of the sight and feel of this place. There is much to explore: Piškera, a good spot to anchor in a fairly busy bay; Lavsa, with firm anchorage and some fishermen's houses breaking the solitude; Levrnaka with a few holiday houses and a lovely beach for bathing; and there are others. This is rocky landscape, desert crags rising a little way out of the water, with 125 islands scattered over a stretch of about twenty miles opening on to the Adriatic. With a few fig and olive trees and stunted vines, it is now a national park which is carefully and lovingly protected, and one of the many things to be admired in Yugoslavia. In summer, it is possible to rent a small cottage equipped with a water tank and gas or oil lighting. Extreme care is needed over navigation here, with the aid of very detailed charts. There are plenty of good places to shelter from the winds, but one must not forget the possibility of dangerous strong currents where the channels are narrower. Leaving the Kornati islands behind us, we head for

WIND CONDITIONS

The prevailing wind in the Adriatic is the bora (NE): a dry, boisterous, sometimes raging wind which forms when masses of cold continental air meet up on the mountains behind the coast with the warmer air coming from the sea.

The bora blows up suddenly without any prior warning, or perhaps preceded by just a few splashes of foam from no fixed direction: a light bora, if it is in a clear sky; a heavy bora, if there are rain clouds. It can be a very useful wind if it stabilizes at around force 3–4, but it can also be quite overpowering, especially in the Gulf of Trieste, in the notorious Kvarner Gulf, and farther down towards Senj, around Zara, in various straits and dangerous channels between Šibenik and Split and south again in the Gulf of Kotor. It causes a very sharp drop in pressure and short, steep waves which are a real problem for boats under 9 m (30 ft). If you are in the open sea and the bora blows from a direction between north and east, it will blow you farther out. This wind can also be very dangerous inside the channels: it whips up foam and spray turning the sea white, and should never be underestimated either when sailing or at anchor, or even when the boat is in harbour.

The sirocco (SE) is a good wind if you are travelling up from the south. Very good progress can be made with the sails slack, riding the great waves that come up from the southern Adriatic. But if you are travelling down from the north it can cause difficulties. A humid wind, nearly always heralded by choppy seas and dark cloud formations, it can last for several days, during which time it will scarcely be worth leaving harbour.

Last comes the mistral (NW). In good, stable weather, it gets up well into the morning and blows until mid afternoon, giving way to calm before sunset and night. It is rarely strong in summer but it is as well to be wary of it.

A detail from the doorway of the Cathedral of St James in Šibenik. The architecture is the result of the fusion of Gothic and Renaissance forms in a style that is typically Yugoslav.

land, crossing the vast internal sea as far as Šibenik (23 nm) and leaving to starboard the last islands which act as a border to this stretch of Dalmatia. Zlarin, with its little harbour surrounded by a picturesque village, would be a good place to stop, but on this occasion we bypass it until we come to the great, solitary fortress which guards the entrance to the narrow channel just before Sibenik.

The mooring along the quay in this large inlet, which is a long way in and complicated, is not of the best; or rather it is a first-rate shelter, but very much an active commercial port. The magnificent old town, with its gleaming streets of polished stone, reflects the Venetian influence. The Venetian Republic's dominion here lasted nearly four centuries, leaving various monuments including the outstanding cathedral of St James with its elaborately engraved doorway and rows of heads jutting out of the side walls: a staggering procession of faces with the most varied expressions, frozen in time. It is perhaps the truest record of all the Venetians, Turks, barbarians, Greeks and others who passed through here, swept along by history. Around the town there are alleyways, warehouses, Venetian-style houses and magnificent, silent courtyards just off the bustling streets. By this time you will have seen many stone lions in the places already visited, but perhaps those of Šibenik are among the best examples of the Venetian presence: there are exquisite ones, with curly manes that could almost be wigs, and on the balustrade of the church of St John the Baptist you can see the weariest, most defeated and feeble lion imaginable. Even a republic strong with a thousand years of freedom, falls in the end like a stricken lion. The Roman Scardona, now Skradin, can be reached by sailing up the bends of the Krka river for about 8 miles. Travelling deep into the hinterland, one comes out into a veritable lake. This is Lake Prokljan, with deep gorges and a complex of 17 waterfalls the highest of which has a 45-m (148-ft) drop. Casting anchor in a small mountain lake, the sea is almost forgotten, and the boat seems almost incongruous.

From Šibenik to Trogir   33 nm

One more stretch of channel, beyond Šibenik with the island of Zlarin to starboard, then due south until

HISTORY: A COMPLEX BACKGROUND

Yugoslavia's unique geographical position, making it a thoroughfare between east and west, is reflected in a complex history, where there has always been opportunity for conquest, profit and power, and where nature, although lavish with beauty, has often been miserly in its distribution of material resources.

The history is an ancient one. The charming seaside resort of Cavtat, for example, built on a tiny promontory, has Greek origins and was the famous Roman settlement of Epidaurum. The Venetians ruled here for centuries at the time of The Most Serene Republic, their naval convoys regularly travelling along the Istrian and Dalmatian coasts, calling at these very well equipped ports. Many of the crewmen came from this area and not just oarsmen who would row the Venetian galleys, for at Perast, now a little village in the Gulf of Kotor (illustrated), there was a famous academy which was able to supply the navy with great admirals and navigators. At that time the Adriatic was known as the Gulf of Venice, and it is important to bear this historical connection in mind when travelling around, since it explains the widespread Venetian influence which is an integral part of Yugoslavia. This influence is particularly striking to the north, in Istria. Further south, the Venetian influence becomes more diluted, although it never disappears altogether.

As you step ashore at many places along the coast, it is worth remembering the existence of various layers of history, and the many upheavals through the ages which saw the supremacy of the Turks followed by that of the Austrians, the French and the Venetians. More recently, in the early twentieth century, Italy sought to recover those parts of Yugoslavia that had formerly been Italian, many Italians having been born in those neighbouring regions that now came under foreign rule. It was a fantasy, an implausible dream to recreate a former empire. Yugoslavia as a nation in its own right was created at the end of the First World War, uniting people who in some instances had very different interests and centuries-old traditions. This has resulted in a country of marked contradictions and the consequences of this background are evident to this day. The sensitive traveller will be aware of this heritage, and will feel it all around him in the places he visits. A sailing holiday can thus turn into a richly rewarding voyage of historical exploration.

At Rogoznica the most unlikely collection of objects, fished up from the sea, form the personal museum of an old diver who served in the French Navy and liked to call himself Napoleon V.

we pass Cape Ploča. We are now in the open sea, with only a few small islands scattered along a jagged coastline where it would be worth stopping again. If one is in the mood for crowds, then Primošten is the place, a well-known tourist resort with good facilities. Those in search of peace should proceed (for 16 nm) as far as the deep inlet which encloses Rogoznica. It provides excellent shelter and is quite a busy fishing port. The restaurants along the wharf are extremely hospitable. There, scampi unloaded from the fishing boats perhaps only an hour earlier, end up cooked *bužara* style, a delicious recipe. Along the promenade, you may still come across a fascinating museum made up of items collected by an old diver during his explorations. There are all manner of things, such as uniforms, flags, medals and all kinds of metal objects retrieved from the seabed, together with other peculiar odds and ends which make up a pleasingly offbeat collection. He waits for passers-by, invites them in and, in exchange for a small entrance fee, regales them with sea stories. Next we come to Cape Ploča, once feared by sailors because they were no longer completely sheltered here, as they had been further north by the islands we have just visited. Beyond the cape is another archipelago, but for the time being, we will stop at Trogir (17 nm),

Opposite: the natural harbour of Pučišća, divided into two arms and situated at the innermost part of a bay on Brač, the largest island in Dalmatia, famous for the export of white stone.

Approaching Trogir from the sea, the first sight to greet you is that of the elegant battlements of the Kastel Kamerlengo. This carefully preserved ancient walled city is one of the most interesting places to visit in the whole of Dalmatia.

in the lee of Ciovo Island. Now that it has been made into an excellent tourist port it has become an even more attractive place to visit, but it is in any case one of the most interesting places for those wishing to see the best monuments in Dalmatia. Trogir was Greek in origin, then Roman, then Byzantine. It was ruled by Odoacer (the first barbarian ruler of Italy), then it was free, then Hungarian or Venetian in turn. There is fine artistic evidence of this complex history.

It is a pleasure to be greeted by the elegant battlements of the Kastel Kamerlengo, and even more enjoyable to walk around the walled city. Trogir is a small town, with a dense network of narrow streets full of delightful glimpses of great artistry, and pervaded with a wonderfully peaceful atmosphere. However, its architectural importance lies in the traces of a flourishing artistic talent which includes Roman, Venetian Gothic and even pre-Renaissance elements. The main square is extremely elegant and St Lawrence Cathedral, looking on to it, is undoubtedly the finest expression of the Dalmatian Romanesque style; note the portal, the work of Master Radovan, which is exceptionally beautiful.

Dalmatia has an outstanding architectural heritage and those who maintain that it is only the result of Venetian rule are very much misguided; of course the Venetian Republic left a deep impression on the area, but it would not be fair to view Dalmatian art as purely reflecting Venetian art. Italian and Slavonic artists worked here, skilled stone masons who produced unique creations. It is no exaggeration to claim that European art cannot be fully understood without having seen its treatment in Dalmatia.

From Trogir to Korčula   60 nm

In northern and central Dalmatia one had the impression of sailing through a sea of islands. Here, however, the archipelago thins out into a few big land masses and, with no further intricate routes offering opportunities to explore secret places, the sea begins to assert its mastery once again. There are currents to be negotiated here, and sudden gusts of wind between the broad channels. Sailing close to the wind in a fresh breeze is a great pleasure and extremely satisfying.

Those who feel like experiencing the hustle and

bustle of a big city should stop at Split, the second largest port in Yugoslavia, where they will find one of the best tourist marinas. Those who prefer less crowded areas should carry on to Hvar. Behind us we leave the island of Šolta, with a series of attractive and peaceful bays, and the island of Brač, the third largest in the Adriatic and once famous for its dazzling white marble, which was quarried since Roman times. Also at Brač we find Vidova Gora, the

This building overlooking the harbour at Hvar was once an arsenal, and is an example of the Venetian influence on this town. Hvar is noted for its mild climate.

highest mountain in the Dalmatian islands at 778 m (2,552 ft). At Milna there is a new marina surrounded by an unspoiled fishing village.

The next stop is Hvar (27 nm), an island with an exceptionally good climate, reputedly enjoying 2,700 hours of sunshine a year. Fragrant with the perfume of wild flowers, much cultivated and very green, it has been dubbed the "Madeira of the Adriatic." The town of Hvar is a busy tourist resort with a number of outstanding monuments and an atmosphere unmistakably flavoured by the historical Venetian influence.

This leaves Korčula, another large island which we almost completely circumnavigate until we reach the splendid little town of the same name (33 nm), built

on a tiny isthmus. It is better not to moor at the main jetty which is unprotected in bad weather, but to go round the town straight into Luka, which is well sheltered from all winds and where the water is still quite clean.

There is something special and singularly beautiful about Korčula, making it perhaps the most precious jewel in the whole Adriatic. Small and extremely well preserved, it is a proud little town imbued with an enchanted atmosphere. The main church, dedicated to St Mark, is richly decorated in Apulian Gothic style; gargoyles, long-nosed creatures, and an abundance of fruit. The Bishop's Palace nearby has a museum with many fine exhibits and is also worth a visit.

Opposite: the tower with the winged lion testifies to the fact that the city of Korčula once came under Venetian rule. Today it is one of the most enchanting places in the Adriatic.
Below: sailing with the spinnaker in a calm sea.

Overleaf: from above, Dubrovnik is covered by a red mass of roofs dating from the Middle Ages and the Renaissance, with a profusion of chimneys and balconies.

Above: the old port of Dubrovnik crowded with fishing boats and pleasure craft. In the past, the great sailing ships that traded all over Europe would dock here.
Below: the bell tower of the Dominican convent built in 1315.

From Korčula to Dubrovnik   46 nm

On leaving Korčula, the islands, a constant and familiar presence along our route, thin out and disappear. To port, we leave the long peninsula of Pelješac, joined to the mainland by a very thin strip; to starboard, Mljet glides by. At its northern end is Polače, with a wonderful, unspoiled bay, sheltered from all the winds. There are few facilities here, so it is best to moor in Rogač bay and enjoy its crystal waters and tranquil solitude.

The archipelago ends. The bows of our vessel point towards Dubrovnik. In the distance the grey of the imposing walls stands out against the colours of the background. Seeing the far-off city takes one back centuries, to the time when the sea belonged to wind and sail, to the pirates, to the Turks and to the equally fierce Venetians. The Republic of Ragusa (Dubrovnik's former name) was also mighty, free and wealthy. It, too, took part in Mediterranean trade with a few other powerful states. The city is built on a small isthmus and is still surrounded by its original walls. Within them, despite a great deal of destruction due to natural causes and wars, it has still managed to retain its former image. Walking along the Stradun, the main street which stretches through the old town center, one marvels at how the centuries-old atmosphere has remained virtually intact. It is a beautiful city, one of Yugoslavia's most precious jewels, proud of an illustrious past and today a thriving tourist center. It will be difficult to find a mooring in port because it is so popular in summer, although the new marina should solve the problem. Dubrovnik is quite simply worth the entire journey.

There have been many staggeringly beautiful moments on our journey, each new discovery more exciting than the last, proving that Dalmatia, with its extraordinary atmosphere, is undoubtedly one of the most captivating places in the world. We have combined the pleasure of its discovery with that of sailing in the unpolluted waters of the Mediterranean. While one could easily travel to Dubrovnik by air, it is so much more rewarding to discover it slowly by sea, gradually adapting to the daily changes in the climate and the landscape.

The Stradun, also known as the Placa, is a road dividing the city of Dubrovnik in two. Created in the twelfth century by filling in a canal, it was covered by its gleaming pavement in 1468. Today, it is a famous place to stroll and shop.

From Dubrovnik to Kotor   44 nm

In many ways Dubrovnik is a good place to end the journey. The archipelago which has been such an important feature in our itinerary ends here and there is little left to see along the coast. But for those who are not satisfied with just the cruise and wish to really learn about such a beautiful and interesting country as Yugoslavia, then it is worth going as far as Kotor. A deep fjord cuts into the coast about 16 nm inland. The high mountains flanking it on either side make it particularly impressive. This is Kotor Fjord (28 nm), the largest natural harbour in Europe used today, as in the past, as a major naval base. On entering the fjord, you must be very careful to follow the special Yugoslav laws governing sailing here. The first place we come to is Hercegnovski Zaliv, where the formalities of entering and leaving Yugoslavia can be dealt with. Proceeding through the mountains, we continue as far as Perast, a tiny village clinging to a hillside, that was long ago a great naval academy. Curiously enough, it resisted the Turks for centuries, and it was also the last place to free itself by force from Venetian rule when the Venetian Republic finally foundered in 1797. Kotor stands at the foot of a 1,759-m (5,770-ft) mountain at the end of the fjord and is interesting because of its close links with Islamic culture. Its hinterland is worth exploring, and a bus ride will take you to breathtaking countryside that is very different from what we have already seen. We are now in Montenegro, a wild, bewitching land where the everyday world seems far removed.

Below: there are two tiny islands in the Gulf of Kotor: Sveti Djordje (right), with a Benedictine monastery, and Skrpjela (left), founded in the seventeenth century.

SAILING AROUND THE ISLANDS

In summer there is not much wind in the Adriatic, particularly in the northern and central areas. However, there are also fine sailing days along the Yugoslavian side, particularly in the channels, where all the strength of the wind can be felt while the sea remains almost flat. Sailors should nevertheless always be vigilant and work out their exact position with the aid of charts. There are myriad islands, often difficult to distinguish by shape alone. The channels are very broad, but shoals and rocks are quite frequent. The passages should be studied in detail and it is advisable to seek expert advice on them, because currents can develop which could prove too strong for the auxiliary motor of a sailing vessel. Lighthouses, beacons and other signals are very reliable and clear indicators of position, and due attention should be paid to them.

The Adriatic sea presents many peculiarities, being very long and rather narrow, so that shoals as well as tides have to be taken into account. It cuts deep into a landscape that is particularly complex from an orographic point of view, and which makes it very hard to obtain truly reliable meteorological information. A constant current travels up the Slavonic coast and then down the Italian one, usually at the speed of about half a knot. If there are changes in tide, wind and pressure, however, the current can reach as much as 3 knots. Sailing around these islands is an unforgettable experience. They form a world apart, which is full of charm and interesting places to discover, but which can also cause ruthless damage. While sailing, it is always a good idea to note the routes that will lead you to emergency shelter, because the boat traffic is very heavy and harbours are crowded, often with inexperienced people who easily become nervous at the first sign of danger: in harbour the anchor does not always hold; sometimes it gets caught up in the ropes; the boats are often too close together, and so on. One final piece of advice which can be useful for finding the best shelter while others are struggling to anchor in the wrong places: remember that all winds end up as the bora. Sometimes the sirocco blows up, usually heralded by obvious meteorological signs. However, the powerful, blustery winds characteristic of this area nearly always stabilize into a north–north-easterly wind.

THE CYCLADES

Kalamaki–Kea–Syros–Mykonos–Paros–Thira–Astipalaia

An expanse of sea strewn with chains of islands nestling so close to one another you could easily imagine yourself on the calmest of salt lakes. We are in the south of the Aegean Sea, the cradle of civilization, where for thousands of years myths and legends have been woven around the natural beauty of its waters. The sea has been linked to the history of man since time immemorial. It is this lure of the past which inspires us to follow routes that have remained unchanged over the centuries, travelling from the Cyclades islands, the archipelago encircling the sacred island of Delos, the land of Apollo, to the Dodecanese, a dozen or so islands scattered off the Turkish coast.

The Aegean is a sailor's paradise: in summer, the meltemi reigns supreme. It is a constant, abundant wind which blows throughout the islands (at speeds of up to 35–40 knots in July and August), coming from the north-east in the Cyclades and from the north-west in the Dodecanese. This wind often makes sailing hard work, but one should not be intimidated by it. The breathtaking beauty of these islands can only be fully appreciated by boat. The sea is usually quite rough in summer, but not as rough as one would expect from the strength of the wind. The sprinkling of islands within these waters helps to break the roll of the waves so that they never exceed 1–1.5 m (3 ft) in height. At the other times of year the temperature is mild, around 15–20°C (60–70°F), the sea is calm, usually with no wind. The Aegean displays different characteristics over the course of the year but it is always ideal for sailing, drawing one into a fairy-tale world which for thousands of years has welcomed those who love the sea.

Windmills are a typical feature of the Cyclades. Surrounded by deep blue sea and the dazzling white of the houses, they hold their sails up to the wind. Their distinctive, geometric shape is characteristic of Mykonos, one of the most beautiful islands of the entire archipelago.

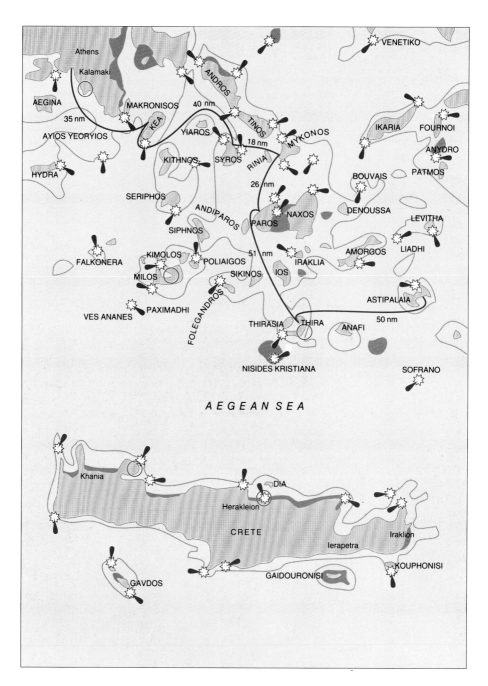

Distance covered: 220 nm.
Average temperatures: July 25°C (75°F); August 27°C (79°F); September 23°C (73°F). Prevailing winds: meltemi, from north-east to north-west, with an average strength of 25–30 knots.

Cartography: British Admiralty: 2836A (general); 1657–1639 (Kalamaki-Sunion-Kea-Syros); 1647 (Mykonos); 1663 (Paros-Naxos-Santorini [Thira]); 3922 (Astipalaia). S.H.O.M. 1259 (Kalamaki-Paros); 1493 (Paros-Astipalaia). Istituto Idrografico Italiano; 438 (general).

Bibliography: Greek Waters Pilot (Imray Laurie Norie & Wilson); Blue Guide to Greece (A. & C. Black, London. W. W. Norton, New York).

From Kalamaki to Astipalaia

Setting out from Kalamaki, a large tourist port a few miles from Athens, we round Cape Sounion, and land at the beautiful, unspoiled island of Kea (first stage: 35 nm). Its slopes are clothed in a colourful mantle of orchards and vines. Our pleasant journey continues with the picturesque, tranquil island of Syros (second stage: 40 nm). The main town, Ermoupolis, is built on the hills overlooking the harbour. It is the administrative capital of the entire archipelago of the Cyclades. An army of windmills stand guard over Mykonos, the liveliest island in Greece with the highest number of nightspots. Mykonos (third stage: 18 nm), is reached by sailing along the beautiful arm of deep blue sea bound to the north by the island of Tinos and to the south, by Rinia and Delos. The breeze which usually blows from the north-east should be enough to carry us to the island of Paros (fourth stage: 26 nm). Its luscious, verdant appearance and the apparent coolness emanating from its high mountains are extremely seductive. The island of Thira (fifth stage: 51 nm) is a haven more often dreamt of than experienced. A spellbinding island, with the warmest colours of the

The vivid blue colour of a dome on Thira blends into the blue immensity of sea and sky, with the mustard colour of the arches providing a pleasing contrast.

entire archipelago, it never disappoints its visitors. The approach to the island is a fantastic experience; we are sailing into the crater of a volcano. On all sides tall, dark walls tower over us. Leaving the Cyclades, we put ashore at the first island in the Dodecanese, Astipalaia (sixth stage: 50 nm), which is strikingly different from the other islands we have encountered so far. It is lower on the horizon and with scanter vegetation, but it is also less touristy and thus still retains its authentic local atmosphere. We are nearing the Turkish coast and at this point of our journey we can already detect the eastern flavour which distinguishes all the islands of the Dodecanese.

From Kalamaki to Kea   35 nm

Here we can appreciate the most outstanding feature of the Greek islands, and the one that makes them so popular: the happy marriage of the world of antiquity with an enchanted landscape.

Leaving Kalamaki around midday and coasting the Saronic Peninsula, one can reach Cape Sounion before sunset, when the sun's rays fall across the majestic temple of Poseidon. This temple, which is situated on the promontory, was built in 444 B.C. It dominates the open sea below, and is an impressive sight for all those who sail into the archipelago. Immediately after leaving Cape Sounion, the island of Kea appears on the horizon. The little harbour of Vourkari in the north-west of the island is very welcoming and the little village behind buzzes with life in the summer months.

In the same bay as the harbour, to the south-east, there is the charming beach of Livadhi, famous for octopus fishing. These creatures abound here, and can easily be caught by diving down a few meters. From opposite the harbour, a short walk leads to the remains of a fortified city dating from the Bronze Age. The largest town on the island is Kea, built on the slopes of a 561-m (1,840-ft) high mountain that is

The snowy wake of a motorboat cuts into the rich, solid colour of the sea's surface; ahead lies a multitude of places to be discovered.

6 km (3¾ miles) from the harbour. Not far from here there is a lion carved out of the rock, dating from the sixth–seventh century B.C. A visit to the ruins of the Hagia Marina monastery at the heart of the island provides a good opportunity to enjoy a magnificent view of one of the finest landscapes in Greece.

From Kea to Syros   40 nm

Leaving Kea behind us, the Aegean Sea unfurls in all its rich blue splendour, the misty contours of the islands barely visible in the distance. Passing to the north of the island of Yiaros and heading south towards Syros, one can make out to the left the mountains of Tinos. On 15 August each year, the Feast of the Assumption of the Virgin Mary, Syros becomes a place of pilgrimage. People arrive from all over Greece. The island of Syros is recognizable from the shape of its hills. The main port of Ermoupolis was the most important in Greece before Piraeus was built in 1870. Even today one can see traces of its former grandeur, particularly in the public buildings built in the nineteenth century. This

Below: in the inland valleys of the island of Tinos, the geometric pattern of the ground makes the terraced landscape look like a painting.

island is less popular with foreign tourists and is one of the places where the Greeks themselves prefer to spend their holidays. The town of Ermoupolis is very interesting with its attractive buildings and magnificent Miaoulis Square. Beneath its Neo-Classical arcades numerous cafés and shops teem with life during the summer season. There is ample opportunity to relax here. The sight of the sunset over the broad bay of Ermoupolis can be combined with the pleasure of sampling some typical Greek fare at one of the numerous restaurants along the quay, where one should not fail to try the famous local sweet, *loukoumi* (Turkish Delight). It is worth taking the boat round to the western side of the island, where there are beautiful, virtually deserted beaches. Drop anchor in one of the many bays and enjoy the deep sapphire blue of the sea, the rugged coastline, and the fine sandy beaches. The beach at Finikas in particular should not be missed.

From Syros to Mykonos 18 nm

According to myth, Poseidon, the god of the sea, hurled a massive boulder at the giants; part of this

Overleaf: the little harbour of Delos, the island famous in antiquity for being the birthplace of Apollo and for the erotic games that took place there once a year. Ancient ruins overlook the sparkling, inviting sea of the Cyclades in an unbeatable combination.

GREEK CUISINE

Traditional Greek dishes date from antiquity. Twenty-five centuries ago, the inhabitants of this country already knew how to combine different ingredients to create delicious concoctions, while the rest of Europe confined themselves to roasting meat.

Olive oil and aromatic herbs and spices have always played an important part in the Greek diet. The addition of these ingredients to the various types of meat and particularly fish, which is plentiful in Greece, has created a varied and appetizing cuisine. Greek soil is usually very fertile and produces flavoursome vegetables and delicious fruit.

There are all sorts of interesting dishes to try, from appetizers to sweets, alternating unusual flavours with other more traditional ones. A glass of ouzo, the anise liqueur which is diluted with water, and a selection of appetizers open the typical Greek meal. Try "tiropitakia" (pastry filled with melted cheese) or "dolmadakia" (rice and minced meat wrapped in vine leaves).

Often served with this course are "tzatsiki," very finely chopped cucumber, yoghurt and garlic, or "taramosalata" (illustrated), a mousse or pâté based on fish roe. Greek meals do not usually include entrées as such; a single main course is served, in which meat and vegetables are often combined, as in "moussaka," made with minced lamb and aubergines. Another classic dish is "souvlaki," or mixed kebabs. To round off the traditional meal, there should be a bottle of retsina on the table. Other traditional Greek foods are the famous Greek olives, feta cheese and yoghurt made from goat's cheese or sheep's cheese, which can be found even on the most remote islands.

mythical boulder is reputed to be Mykonos, which lies to the east of Syros. This island, more than any other, is transformed in summer into a lively and carefree holiday resort. Mykonos has a great deal to offer. The scenery – wild countryside covered with dusky green Mediterranean maquis (shrubby vegetation) – combined with the multicoloured houses of the town of Mykonos, create the perfect balance that only time and nature can achieve. The characteristic windmills silhouetted against the skyline are exposed to the force of the meltemi, which swirls through the lanes of Mykonos. The colourful hustle and bustle of summer are not the sole attractions of Mykonos; the traces of the past are the most striking features of this island. There are over 300 churches on Mykonos, two of the most interesting of which are at Paraportiani and the Paleokastro monastery at the center of the island, near the Venetian fortress of Darga. In order to understand the local history, one should take the time to visit the two museums on the island: the ethnographic museum near Paraportiani Church and the museum of antiquities near the Leto Hotel, full of fascinating archaeological remains from Delos and Rinia. The little port of Mykonos is not an ideal

Above: imposing marble lions, the royal guards of Delos, the sacred island of antiquity.

Below: flowers add bright colourful splashes to the white lanes of Mykonos, a bustling island full of vitality.
Overleaf: the little harbour of the island of Mykonos, surrounded by a sea streaked with different shades of blue.

mooring place when the meltemi blows hard in July
and August: it is better to seek shelter in the Bay of
Ornos, to the south of the island. There, one can
enjoy peace and quiet immersed in beautiful landscape. The water is emerald-green and the low hills
surrounding the bay provide shelter from the wind.
Landing on the beach, you will find all the facilities
you need: restaurants, hotels, and buses or taxis into
the town of Mykonos.

As though the wealth of architectural interest and
variety of things to do were not enough, the island
of Mykonos is also of particular interest to those
interested in wildlife. Just off the coast is the little
island of Tragonissi, which is one of the last refuges
of the few surviving seal colonies in the
Mediterranean.

The chief attraction of this little archipelago is the
island of Delos, famous in antiquity for the erotic
games that were held there once a year, and for being
the birthplace of Apollo. One can reach it by caique
(local boat) from the port of Mykonos, or in your
own vessel, bearing in mind, however, that there are
treacherous shoals there.

There is very little room to moor in the tiny harbour of Delos and you will only have until 3 pm to
visit the remains of the legendary temples of the
ancient Greeks, including the stone lions which stand
guard over the island. After 3 pm, you are not
allowed to stop at or near the island, which is only
inhabited by the custodians of the archaeological
sites and the curator of the museum.

From Mykonos to Paros   26 nm

Our intellect having been stimulated by a glimpse
into antiquity on Delos and our desire for relaxation
and entertainment satisfied on Mykonos, we now
approach the largest islands of the Cyclades: Paros
and Naxos. These lie at the heart of the archipelago
and dominate all the other islands with their mountains, which are the highest in the Cyclades. At
Paros, we disembark at the port of Paroikia, the
capital in the north-west of the island. From a distance one can pick out its characteristic white houses.
You will find it a busy commercial center in summer,
and the archaeological museum well worth a visit.

For a more peaceful spot, it is better to sail round
to the north of the island, into the Bay of Naoussa, a

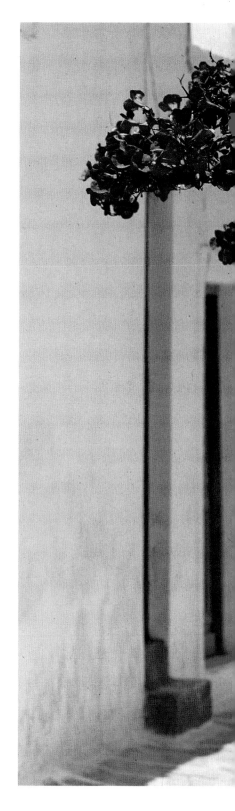

ARCHAEOLOGY AT PAROS

The little archaeological museum at Paroikia houses many interesting items including the wingless Nike – the ancient Greek goddess of victory – dating from the fifth century B.C., and the famous chronological tablet of 263 B.C. giving the apocryphal date of the birth of Homer. The tablet is carved out of the precious white marble which made the island into a wealthy, thriving commercial center in antiquity. One can still visit the pits where it was quarried (the marble chips inside are said to bring good luck). The last marble quarried there was for Napoleon's tomb.

The Byzantine church of Ekaton-Dapyliani, Our Lady of the Hundred Doors, was built near the port in the sixth century A.D. It has a composite structure including a large church dedicated to the Virgin Mary, a smaller one dedicated to St Nicholas, and a baptistery in the shape of a cross, with steps leading down to the water. Contrary to what its name suggests, it has probably more than a hundred doors if you take into account all the apertures, including arches and windows. The two sanctuaries of Aphrodite and Apollo, to the north of the city on the slopes of Mount Koumados, should also be visited. An interesting feature of the island is the Convent of Christos Tou Dassou, famous for its butterfly garden, where only women are admitted. It could almost be in retaliation to the famous Greek monastery of Mount Athos, where only men have access.

Colour is a vital element in the beauty of Mykonos. Here the light blue of the doors contrasts effectively with the scarlet flowers in a sun-kissed lane.

MILOS

After some strenuous sailing, holding steady in the fresh breeze which blows in this part of the Cyclades, it is a great relief to enter the deep anchorage of Milos, an island of volcanic origin and one of the most attractive and safest havens in the whole of Greece. The famous statue of Venus (150 B.C.), found here in 1820 and now housed in the Louvre, has turned Milos into a symbol of the Greek islands. This image is further enhanced by the beauty of its coastline with its many unspoilt beaches. Good beaches may be found on the little islands of Kimolos and Polynos. The latter is completely un-inhabited and its volcanic origins give it a rather somber atmosphere.

Before arriving at Milos it is worth making a brief visit to the island of Siphnos, famous for its oil and ceramics. The old capital, Kastro, is characterized by an intricate geometrical pattern of bridges which connect the upper floors of many of its houses, creating interesting architectural effects.

picturesque fishing village which has retained its local traditions. The bay is very broad and, although not entirely protected from the meltemi, has some good moorings. The little uninhabited islands, which are numerous in this stretch of water, provide particularly good moorings. Opposite Naoussa is the anchorage of Kolimbithres. Its dazzling white sandy bottom reflects the sun's rays on to the surface of the sea, creating sparkling effects.

Moving to the west of the island of Paros, you can travel by caique to the tiny island of Antiparos where, apart from enjoying beautiful empty beaches, it is possible to visit a grotto 70 m (230 ft) underground. The trip to the grotto involves a pleasant ride on a mule. A flight of steps takes us down into the bowels of the earth, to a cavern dripping with stalactites.

Like Theseus following "Ariadne's thread" to find his way out of the Minotaur's labyrinth, we reach Naxos. According to Greek mythology, Theseus and Ariadne, having defeated the Minotaur at Crete, set sail for Athens, disembarking at Naxos. After they had eaten and rested, Theseus departed, abandoning his consort. She soon found consolation in Dionysus, the god of wine. Indeed, Naxos is famous for its abundant vegetation and valleys studded with vineyards, orchards and olive groves. It is rare to find such a fertile landscape in the Cyclades. The city of

Naxos is the capital of the island, which for a long time was ruled by the Venetians. The Venetian influence can still be seen today in the Dukes' Palace situated at the top of the town, with its main tower clearly visible from the sea along our route. This friendly port has two very interesting features: the ruins of the Temple of Apollo, dating from the sixth century B.C., and the Myrtidiotissa chapel built on a tiny islet a few yards from the quay. The whole island

Opposite: a glimpse of Paroikia, a town on the island of Paros.

Below: the intricate network of buildings that make up the town of Naxos is dominated by the Dukes' Palace, seen here through the imposing ruins of the sixth-century Temple of Apollo.

is worth exploring, with its many excellent sandy beaches which are often only accessible by sea. To the far north is the little village of Apollona with a colossal, 9-m (30-ft) high unfinished stone statue. The south of the island is certainly the most tranquil area and it is well sheltered from the meltemi. After dropping anchor in one of the numerous bays, you can enjoy a view of citrus groves, whose leaves are used to prepare the delicious local liqueur, Citron.

From Paros to Thira   51 nm

Leaving Naxos, we head south through waters of ever deepening blue. To port we pass the island of Ios where, according to Greek mythology, Homer died (it is now a nudist colony), and approach an island shrouded in mystery. The fragile relationship between man and earth can be found in the volcanic island of Thira, formerly Santorini. In the sixteenth century B.C. a terrific eruption destroyed the island and since then the inhabitants have lived under its threat. During the eruption the city was submerged beneath the ash and lava, and a glorious civilization was destroyed. It has now been brought to light thanks to careful excavation. The sea filled the crater and sailing in these waters is very eerie. Some of the results of excavating can be seen in the southern part of the island, where the remains of the Minoan city of Akrotiri, destroyed in 1500 B.C., have been uncovered. These, together with the black and red sheer cliff walls formed by masses of cooled lava surrounding the little central crater, form a dramatic sight. It is this feeling of latent power, austerity and harshness that makes Thira so arresting.

A boat is the perfect vehicle for appreciating the rugged beauty of this island, even though the only mooring place is at Skala, where one must take care not to occupy the spaces reserved for the ferries that berth at the left-hand wharf. The journey from Skala to Thira, the capital of the island, is by cable car or on the traditional mules, which scramble up a tortuous route to a height of 500 m (1,640 ft). Here one really must stop at one of the many terraced restaurants, not just to admire the view, but also to taste one of the famous local wines: the white Atlantis or red Vikteri.

Nea Kaimeni and Palaia Kaimeni are the two uninhabited islands inside the volcano. The first is

ARCHAEOLOGY AT THIRA

Walking through the ruins of Thira, which cover an area 800 m (2,600 ft) long and 150 m (500 ft) deep, you can almost feel transported to the very dawn of civilization. The earliest archaeological evidence of this city dates from the ninth century B.C., with the sanctuary dedicated to the Egyptian deities Anubis and Serapis and the graffiti from the eighth century B.C., recording the names of the young men who danced in honour of the god Apollo. Dances and festivals took place on the "Terrace of the Festivals," one of the oldest religious centers of Doric culture near the remains of the temple built in honour of the god Apollo Karneios.

Before reaching Thira, you can climb up to the monastery of the prophet Elijah at Pirgos, at a height of 584 m (1,916 ft) where there is a good view of the island.

The houses of Thira, built on the edge of the island's volcanic crater.
Overleaf: the island offers many picturesque views. Here, the warm rays of the setting sun envelop the sea, the houses and the church domes in a single embrace. The proximity of the Orient can be clearly sensed.

CRETE

Let us pick up the thread of Ariadne, abandoned by Theseus at Naxos, and follow the trail of that famous myth back to Crete, home of many of the ancient Greek gods and the largest island in the Aegean. In ancient times it was considered a true continent in its own right.

Crete has three different climates: Mediterranean in the northern part, semidesert in the southern part, and mountain at the center. This subdivision reflects the island's geography. The north coast is mild, with many isolated beaches, often impossible to reach by land, such as on the Gramvousa peninsula at the far west of the island. The south coast is high and rocky with a big drop from day to night temperatures. The center of the island is composed of a chain of mountains, the highest peak being Mount Ida (2,450 m/8,038 ft).

Zeus, the king of the gods, is said to have been born in a cave on this mountain. This made Crete a noble and sacred island in the eyes of ordinary mortals.

The island makes its living from the past, from the remains of Crete's former grandeur. An important example is the sumptuous Palace of Knossos at Herakleion. There are also remains of the Minoan civilization at Phaestos and the old quarter in the capital city of Khania, where one can visit the Mosque of the Janissaries, dating from the period of Turkish rule. To appreciate the beauty of this island to the full, one should sail along the coast exploring the innumerable sheltered bays, enjoying not just the sea, but the unspoiled nature where there are still many orchid species growing wild.

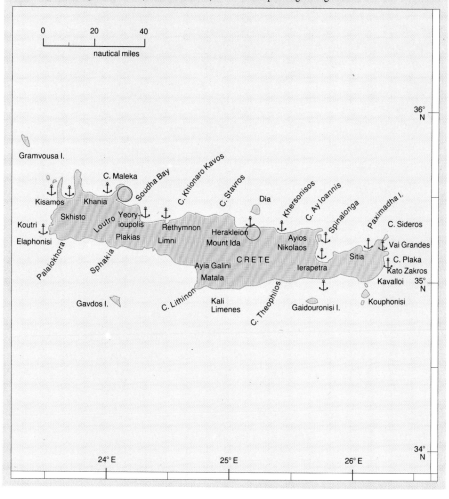

part of the crater itself, whilst the second is a little island which emerged during the eruption of 1925. Mooring in one of the bays on these islands is like entering a primitive world: the rocks of cooled lava, the deep, almost black sea conjure up images of an infernal landscape that remind us yet again that the force of the elements rules here and that man cannot oppose the power of nature.

Paying great attention to the seabed, it is possible to approach a little bay on Palaia Kaimeni which faces on to the channel formed by the two islands. The water here is reddish due to the presence of sulphur and has a temperature of about 25–30°C (75–85°F). Do not be put off from bathing by this weird landscape, for the sulphurous waters are very soothing.

In contrast to the sheer drops within the crater, the external slopes look much more hospitable, particularly in the western part of Thirasia. This crest of land, part of another section of the emergent volcano, forms a second island. A mantle of fertile land covers the gentle slopes with olive groves and vineyards rolling down to the sea. It is not advisable to moor here for the night as there is no protection from the meltemi. However, the eastern part of the island of Thira is sheltered from the wind. It also has

Overleaf: the sails swell under the force of the wind. In the Cyclades, the meltemi blows briskly during the daylight hours, making sailing enjoyable and exciting.

Below: at sunset everything is tinged with yellow. It is a magical moment on the island of Thira. The shadows lengthen, creating wonderful geometrical shapes which slowly melt into the darkness.

good places to swim. There are long, broad beaches with black sand, such as the one at Perissa in the south-east, which is 16 km (10 miles) long. Sailing back up the coast, it is worth casting anchor in the bay opposite ancient Thira, one of the most important archaeological sites in the whole of Greece. There one can see tombs with archaic inscriptions, the remains of the fortified town, ruins and temples; evidence of the numerous civilizations that have left their mark on this mysterious and intriguing island.

From Thira to Astipalaia   50 nm

Sailing deeper into the heart of the Aegean, we leave

Below: the island of Astipalaia in the Dodecanese archipelago displays a striking landscape. Deep inlets carry the vivid blue of the sea into a land scorched by the sun, creating extraordinary colour contrasts.

the Cyclades behind to encounter Astipalaia, the first island in the Dodecanese archipelago, about 170 miles from Piraeus and 90 from Rhodes. From a distance it looks like two separate islands, and only on drawing nearer can one make out an isthmus joining them. This thin sliver of land is like a lifeline protecting the inhabitants from the force of the wind and sea. Astipalaia was famous in the past for the abundance of fish around its shores and even today, fishing is the main livelihood of the people who live there. The island also provides innumerable opportunities for those who enjoy fishing as a hobby. It is easy to find large quantities of fish along its ragged coastline and near the little islands of Kunupia and

Overleaf: light blue, dark blue and white; through the rigid geometrical shapes of a wall, we follow the change in colour from the deep blue of the sea to the light blue shades of the sky.

On page 67: a pelican wanders freely through the narrow streets of Mykonos. In the Cyclades man jealously preserves a simple lifestyle which is still closely in touch with nature.

Kutzomiti. These, together with Ligno and Kondro, form a miniature archipelago within the broad, sheltered bay which the town of Maltezana overlooks.

Landing at Skala, we will be immediately aware of how different this island is from those already encountered on our journey. Far from the busy tourist routes and without the bustle which is off-putting to those in search of relaxation, Astipalaia has a timeless atmosphere. Its links with the past are strengthened by traditions thousands of years old. The port of Skala is used almost exclusively by local fishermen and the quay is busy with sailors, not tourists, disentangling colourful fishing nets and carrying boxes of fresh fish. The town is dominated by the thirteenth-century Venetian Quirini fortress, which has recently been restored. Nearby is the church of the Madonna of the Fortress, one of the loveliest in the Dodecanese. Its iconostasis – a screen symbolically separating the faithful from God – is completely covered in gold filigree. Sailing along the coast, there are innumerable bays surrounded by small, barren hills. The most attractive is undoubtedly that of Vathy, in the north of the island. After carefully negotiating a narrow strait, one reaches a beautiful expanse of water which is so sheltered and secluded that it seems like a small lake. Dropping anchor and going for a swim in one of these bays is like stepping into a dream world. In this idyllic setting modern civilization seems very remote.

RELIGIOUS FESTIVAL AT TINOS AND ASTIPALAIA

The Feast of the Assumption of the Virgin Mary, on 15 August, is an important date for most of the Greek people. It is a particularly important occasion at Tinos since an icon of the Madonna was found there in 1922, which was immediately believed to have miraculous properties.

Since then, more and more pilgrims have flocked to the church of Panayia Evanghelistria, which was specially built to celebrate this festival following the discovery of the icon.

On this feast day the main road from the harbour to the sanctuary is given over entirely to the procession of the faithful, while the other roads are lined with shops and stalls selling little bottles of holy water, incense, relics, ex-votos and other religious artefacts.

The inhabitants of the island are very loyal to their traditions. There is an age-old custom of building decorative dovecotes, which can be found throughout the island. There is no clear explanation for this tradition although some guide books attribute it to a Venetian vogue for dove-keeping combined with a craze for tower building which swept through Italy during the early years of the Most Serene Republic.

The Feast of the Assumption of the Virgin is also celebrated at Astipalaia in the Dodecanese, at the Panayia Portaitissa Convent near the capital, Skala. The women wear traditional costume and music is played on local instruments such as the "santuri" and "lagumi." This is a thoroughly enjoyable occasion for both inhabitants and visitors who may wish to take part. Dancing continues until dawn, and succulent local dishes based on vegetables, cheese and fish are offered to all participants.

TURKEY

LYCIA

Marmaris–Ekinçik Liman–Wall Bay–Fethiye–Ölü Deniz –Kalkan–Kaş–Gökkaya–Çineviz Liman–Antalya

A rugged coastline covered in thick vegetation with a number of inviting bays and a clear blue-green sea that is the mighty custodian of undiscovered archaeological secrets. We are in Turkey, sailing alongside a strip of land, Caria, which faces on to the Aegean Sea opposite the Dodecanese archipelago. It continues with Lycia, opening out into the easternmost basin of the Mediterranean, a stretch of water that has fostered trade between east and west since ancient times.

The history of this land spans thousands of years and has been shaped by four different cultures (Hittite, Byzantine, Graeco-Roman and Ottoman). Its interest derives from its spectacular scenery and from the strong Islamic influence that is central to the Turkish way of life.

Leaving Marmaris, one is struck by the rich, green vegetation which colours the entire coastline, dotted here and there with white houses. The coast is deeply indented as far as Ekinçik Liman, where it becomes softer and less craggy towards the mouth of the Koycegiz river, facing the island of Delikada.

Inside the Gulf of Fethiye, the coast regains its tortuous character, the lush green hills and calm blue sea inspiring a feeling of tranquillity. Wall Bay, the island of Tersane and the city of Fethiye are just some of the places which make this gulf a paradise for sailors. Nature has been lavish with its beauty along this stretch of coast. The bay of Ölü Deniz is one of these gems where sea and land are in perfect harmony. Continuing towards Kalkan, we sail past a rough shore known as the Seven Capes. Against this

The Lycian coast basks in the shade of fragrant Aleppo pines. The water is so deep that one has to use their sturdy trunks as mooring posts. It is essential to be equipped with very long mooring ropes.

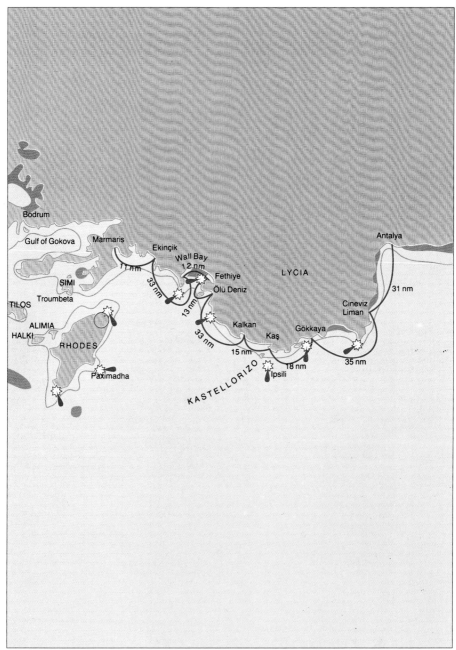

Distance covered: 211 nm.
Average temperatures: spring 20°C (70°F) and summer 27°C (79°F).
Prevailing winds: meltemi from June to September, up to 35 knots. Sea breezes in late afternoon.
Cartography: British Admiralty: 236 (Bodrum-Antalya); 1545 (Marmaris); 1886 (Ekinçik-Liman-Fethiye); 1604 (Gulf of Gökova); French S.H.O.M.: 1478 (Bodrum-Marmaris); 1484 (Marmaris-Gökkaya); 6993 (Gökkaya-Antalya); Istituto Idrografico Italiano: 438 (general).
Bibliography: Turkish Water Pilot (Imray Laurie Norie & Wilson); Turkey and the Dodecanese Cruising Pilot, Robin Petherbridge (Aldard Coles Ltd); Blue Guide to Turkey (A. & C. Black, London. W. W. Norton, New York).

unkempt backdrop are the ruins of Xanthos and Patara, evidence of Turkey's illustrious past. The voyage continues eastwards to the little Greek island of Kastellorizo, a peaceful spot. Kaş, on the Turkish coast, is a few kilometers away. This stretch of coast is full of small bays, long fjords which cut into the land with its thick blanket of vegetation, and small islands. All this gives a warm friendly atmosphere to the area where the great bay of Uçagiz and Gökkaya opens up, in front of the island of Kekova. The city of Finike is the last stop before the coast turns northwards to form the great Gulf of Antalya. The city of Antalya lies in the curve of this bay. A rich eastern atmosphere pervades its squares, houses and mosques. A visit to this city will ensure happy memories of the Turkish coast and leave one with the desire to return and rediscover one of the most entrancing areas of the Mediterranean.

A view of Marmaris harbour, with local caiques and pleasure boats. Marmaris is one of the main charter resorts in Turkey.

GULF OF GÖKOVA

The whole of the Turkish coastline is worth exploring. It is awash with beauty and history. This is particularly true of the Gulf of Gökova, which extends eastwards for 50 miles opposite the Greek island of Kos. The northern side of the entrance to the gulf is dominated by the town of Bodrum (illustrated). Known in ancient times as Halicarnassus, it is famous for being the birthplace of the historian Herodotus. It was also the site of one of the seven wonders of the world – the original *mausoleum* – a magnificent tomb built in honour of King Mausolus, which has now disappeared. The Bodrum of today, the capital of Caria, is an ideal starting-point from which to explore the Gulf of Gökova. The well-protected and well-equipped harbour lies in front of a picturesque town with narrow winding streets. There are plenty of good restaurants with terraces overlooking the sea, where one can sit and drink raki, the local anise-flavoured spirit.

The Crusader Castle of St Peter, built by the Knights of Rhodes in 1402, is a masterpiece of military architecture, still in perfect condition. It contains an interesting museum of marine archaeology which is the only one of its kind.

A few small deserted bays face on to the gulf, protected from behind by hills and a number of mountains. It is as though nature had reserved these small pockets of unspoilt beauty exclusively for those who approach them by boat. Cast anchor and savour the tranquillity, or enjoy a relaxing swim. This is a captivating shoreline which offers innumerable safe shelters from the wind and sea. At the far eastern end of the gulf lies

the bay of Akbuk, where sparkling blue waters lap the feet of rocky mountains cloaked in pine and olive trees. Visit Castle (or Cleopatra) island in the Sehir archipelago, and stroll among the gnarled olive trees. Look around the ruins of a Hellenistic city, half-buried by the lush vegetation. Further along there is an immaculate white beach where you can swim in the brilliant clear water. The seven islands of Yedi Adalari, scattered halfway across the southern coast, suggest a gulf within a gulf. A narrow stretch of sea reaches inland for about half a kilometer. It is a narrow opening, completely surrounded by land, making it seem like an inland lake.

Shrubs, pines and olive trees along the shores form a tapestry of green that is reflected in the still, clear water. The only inhabitants of the bay are blue-coloured fish and the occasional heron, which still manage to live undisturbed in this little paradise. At the end of the southern coast is the ancient Knidos, one of the six cities of the Dorian confederacy. A narrow isthmus separates the old harbour from the one now in use which does not offer very good shelter. The ruins of the city are scattered over the promontory and the land to the north. These are worth visiting, particularly for the famous statue of Aphrodite dating from the fourth century B.C. Many legends are attached to this statue, nearly all focusing on the goddess's sensuality, but the one most widely believed attributes her with the power of bringing good luck to all sailors who go to see her.

From Marmaris to Ekinçik Liman   21 nm

The Orient starts here: the city of Marmaris is a bustling bazaar, where exotic colours and aromas mingle with the inhabitants thronging the narrow streets, creating an atmosphere which immediately captivates the tourist. The stalls are laden with fresh fruit and vegetables, and traders press visitors to purchase the delicious pine honey, the most famous local product. All this vitality and colour make the city an excellent starting point for a cruise along the Lycian coast. Marmaris lies at the center of a broad, triangular bay blocked to the south by a peninsula protecting it from the wind and sea. This stretch of water is ideal for sailing. The first stretch will be smooth, surrounded by high mountains covered in a thick blanket of woodland. Carried by the light wind which normally blows along this part of the coast, we leave the bay of Marmaris and take to the open sea as far as the mouth of the Koycegiz river, the first leg of our journey. The river flows gently towards the sea, with broad, sinuous curves in the final part of its journey. A good way of exploring the river is by tender (the small vessel used for going ashore) or better still, by one of the little boats that may be hired from the locals who will be happy to act as a guide. Real treasures are concealed along the banks of this river. The ancient inhabitants of Lycia carved their tombs out of the cliffs, in eternal memory of their dead. These stately monuments, with columns obviously influenced by Ionic art, are clearly visible halfway up the tall, vertical rock face rising from the river bank. Continuing upstream, herons, hawks and kingfishers may be spotted among the reed beds, and even a few large turtles, which are still able to breed in the peace and quiet of this unspoiled oasis. About five miles up river, one can go ashore and visit the ruins of the ancient city of Caunos. It is a twenty-minute walk, but well worth the effort. There are the remains of a medieval fortress built on a little hill and, close by, a magnificent Roman amphitheater with a seating capacity of 15,000, which has survived virtually intact. You will also find a magnificent view of the old port, which is now silted up and connected to the sea by a narrow waterway. After all this activity, it is time for some much-needed refreshment. At Dalyan, a little fishing village built along the river, there is an excellent restaurant serving very

Along the Lycian coast, rugged cliffs alternate with broad, deep bays surrounded by gentle hills covered in luxuriant vegetation.

RHODES

Leaving the city of Marmaris behind us, let us head out to sea, carried by a light meltemi and cut across the short stretch of water which separates the Turkish coast from Rhodes, described as the pearl of the Dodecanese.

Leaving the boat in Mandraki harbour at the north of the island, we step on to Greek soil at Rhodes, the island's capital. Medieval walls surround the ancient heart of the city, which is well preserved, with patches of greenery here and there. Rhodes is famous for the myth of the bronze colossus, the legendary statue of Apollo, one of the Seven Wonders of the World, destroyed by an earthquake in 227 B.C. Rhodes, the ancient city of the Knights (an order established to defend Christianity against the Muslim infidel) shows many traces of this rich past. It has magnificent buildings and monuments to be found by wandering through the narrow streets of the old town center, including the imposing Castle of the Knights of Rhodes. These remind us of the early struggles of Christianity, while the numerous mosques are tangible proof of two centuries of Ottoman rule. The city of Rhodes was designed by Hippodamus of Miletus and boasted one of the most famous schools of art and rhetoric in antiquity. This is the threshold of the Orient. It can be felt by walking along the main street of the old town where a huge bazaar overflows with the many goods produced by the local craftsmen. The air is fragrant with spices and musk.

There are also some very interesting places to visit outside Rhodes. Ten kilometers (6 miles) south of the city, is the spa resort of Kallithea. At the top of Mount Philerimos, 15 km (9 miles) south-west of Rhodes, is the ancient city of Ialysos, which with Lindos and Kamiros, was one of the three Dorian cities. At the foot of the acropolis, built with the foundations of the Temple of Athena and with the ruins of the Byzantine towers, there is a beautiful fountain with Doric columns. It commemorates the flight from the upper city which took place in 1400 B.C. at the time of the massive volcanic eruption on the island of Santorini. History is not Rhodes' only attraction. The entire island is a place of outstanding natural beauty. The southern coast is particularly charming. A few miles from Rhodes is a very wide beach, encircled by a band of shrubs, which slopes down to the sea at a 45° angle.

Continuing south, the coastline becomes sharper and more jagged. At this stage of our journey, we will enter the fairy-tale bay of Lindos (illustrated opposite). It is halfway along the south coast, where the rocks become less steep and the coast more hospitable. On entering the bay, it is best to moor on the right-hand side, the sheer rock face behind offering protection from the wind. Across the water, you can admire the acropolis of Lindos, built on the headland across the bay.

The little village of Lindos lies in the center of the bay. Although it is quite crowded in summer, it is a very beautiful spot to which each prevailing culture, from Turkish to Greek, has contributed its own individual style of architecture. Continuing along this coast, we arrive at Cape Prassonissi at the southern tip of Rhodes. Those wishing to circumnavigate the island should bear in mind that there are often strong winds and a rough sea.

Another interesting place to visit is the Petaloudes valley, about 36 km (22 miles) inland from Rhodes, the home of thousands of multi-coloured butterflies. At rest, they are camouflaged so as to blend perfectly with the leaves. When in flight, it is as though delicate coloured leaves were swirling gracefully through the air.

The absence of built-up areas along the coastline has meant that the natural beauty and clear waters have remained unspoilt.

good fresh fish. If you stay until sunset, you will be rewarded by a stunning natural spectacle. The rock with the Lycian tombs slowly changes colour, assuming even softer and warmer shades. Once back on the boat, it is a good idea to spend the night in the bay of Ekinçik, not far from Delikada island.

From Ekinçik Liman to Wall Bay　　　33 nm

Before leaving the beautiful bay of Ekinçik, take a dip in the sparkling clear water. At the sight of the sheer beauty of the Turkish coast, you cannot but feel in tune with nature and at peace with the rest of the world. The Gulf of Fethiye produces the same feeling of delight and well-being after the exhilaration of sailing in the open sea. The distant coastline (from Cape Disibilmez to Cape Kordoglu) has an irregular appearance: tall white cliffs alternating with long beaches dappled with dark patches of vegetation.

Entering the Gulf of Fethiye from the west, we encounter a series of little islands stretching in a broken chain parallel to the uneven coast of the gulf, creating a series of narrow straits. Entering through one of these channels is to be admitted to a world of almost unearthly tranquillity. One is struck by the perfection of nature's handiwork in providing countless secluded and virtually private landing stages. The sailor will feel an instant affinity with the coastline beckoning him alluringly to further exploration of its inlets and beaches.

Wall Bay is almost circular in shape and is situated at the southernmost point of the gulf, in the bay of Skopea. Its unusual features are the high wall running along the right-hand side and the lush green hills surrounding the entire bay. You will notice the vivid colour and variety of vegetation: Aleppo pines and olive trees crowd all the available space, practically tumbling down into the water. On mooring one is overcome by a feeling of peace. The deep, clear water reveals the beautiful seabed which is well worth exploring. Another superb place to stop is the island of Tersane, which is the Turkish word for shipyard. The anchorage is safe, situated in a deep bay on the north-west side of the island. There was probably a flourishing naval dockyard there in the past, but now there is only a little village inhabited by

THE LYCIAN TOMBS OF FETHIYE

The mastery of Lycian architects is best demonstrated by the tomb at Aminta (pictured left). It was built in the fourth century B.C. during the conquest of Alexander the Great. The Greek influence is evident in the two smooth columns supporting a tympanum carved with a sacred frieze and sun disc. Below the tympanum is a false door. The entrance to the tomb is concealed behind a moveable stone slab at the right of the façade.

On pages 78 and 79: a sandy coastline south of Ekinçik Liman.

Overleaf: view of the Gulf of Fethiye.

Below: from the ruins of ancient Caunos there is a fine view of the mouth of the river Koycegiz and the remains of what used to be the Roman port.

a few peasant families. Further along the shore, at the far end of the bay, there are some ruins of an ancient Byzantine city set among olive and palm trees.

The unspoilt charm of these places is highlighted by the glowing sunsets, when the countryside is bathed in an aura of peace and nature holds absolute sway.

From Wall Bay to Fethiye   12 nm

A peninsula encloses the eastern side of the Gulf of Fethiye, forming a broad bay protected from the winds. The calm waters invite you to enjoy this tranquillity and then to stop at the city of Fethiye at the southern end of the gulf. Before entering the harbour, one can admire the spectacular tombs carved out of the rocks in the Taurus Mountains behind the town. These are the only surviving remains of Telmessus, which in ancient times was the most important trading center of the entire Lycian coast.

The port of Fethiye is an ideal place for replenishing food supplies. Early each morning, the city comes alive with a colourful open-air market where one can find everything, from vegetables to very fresh fish and the delicious local yoghurt. Although the city was badly damaged by an earthquake in 1958, it has still retained much of the charm due to its fascinating history. An archaeological museum houses the treasures that are part of Fethiye's past, including, near the entrance, the trilingual stele of Leto. This block of calcareous stone, 1.35 m (4 ft 4 in) high is inscribed with a religious text dedicated to the gods Kaunios and Arkesimas and prophesying doom on those who infringe the cult. The text must have had considerable influence, as it was inscribed in three languages: Lycian, Greek and Armenian.

About 25 km (15½ miles) from Fethiye, on the road to Ölü Deniz, is the village of Kaya. Consisting of a hundred or so white-washed houses perched on a hillside, it was completely abandoned by its population in 1923, when the entire area was handed over from Greece to Turkey. Walking among the derelict houses, it is as though some catastrophe has recently befallen Kaya, forcing its inhabitants to flee. All the houses lack roofs and the two churches in the village

On pages 84 and 85: the peninsula enclosing the bay of Skopea, where the beautiful anchorage of Wall Bay is situated. A narrow isthmus separates it from the open sea and creates an ideal place for a walk at sunset.

have been stripped by thieves and vandalized. The air of desolation which pervades the houses of Kaya is the result of the troubles between Greece and the Ottoman Empire at the beginning of the twentieth century.

Before leaving Fethiye, one should climb a little way up the slopes of the mountain behind the town, near the rock tombs. There one can see the remains of a Byzantine citadel, including sections of the old city walls. There is also a magnificent view of the entire bay.

From Fethiye to Ölü Deniz   15 nm

The sea here shields a whole treasure house of human history, and it is thanks to its protection that the damage wrought by time is partly kept at bay. Visitors to the island of Gemile will be thrilled by the magnificence of the submerged ruins that the sea has managed to preserve perfectly. The island lies in the bay round from Cape Ilbiz, the last stretch of land in the Gulf of Fethiye. Take care not to be too distracted by the scenery, as there are some hazardous shoals extending from the cape to the island of Karacaoren. Once past this danger, the island of Gemile appears. A broad channel about 200 m (660 ft) long separates it from the coast and it is in this stretch of water that one can see the remains of an ancient Byzantine city, which sank into the sea after an earthquake. It is a strange and breathtaking experience to explore houses, churches and entire streets through the lens of a crystal-clear sea. The safest way to do this is by using the tender, after mooring at the north-west of the island, which is the most sheltered and picturesque area. The port of Gemile was very busy in the past because there was ample fresh water to be had on the island. This water used to be collected in huge tanks which can still be seen near the remains of the Bishop's Palace. The church of St Nicholas, rich in treasures, has an unusual corridor with a vaulted ceiling which leads down towards the sea. This is a peculiar structure, about 100 m (330 ft) long, connecting the beach at the north of the island with the Palace and Church of St Nicholas. It was used by the island's dignitaries who landed at the shore and were able to walk to the palace and church under cover. The above are just two of the island's most interesting archaeological

Below: the ruins of the vaulted passage leading from the Church of St Nicholas on the island of Gemile to the sea.

TURKISH CUISINE

When you hear people in Turkey talk about "luscious lips" and "lady's thighs" or inviting "lady's navels," it is not a ruse to lure the hapless tourist, but the names of some traditional Turkish dishes whose roots go back to the period of Ottoman rule.

To fully appreciate this country's cuisine, one must start with the raki (hors d'oeuvre) course, (illustrated below). This course is a ritual in itself, which can last well into the early hours and even replace the entire meal. There are cold appetizers: black olives; shelled almonds; marinated mackerel and sardines; stuffed vine leaves; stuffed tomatoes, courgettes and peppers; white cheese and yoghurt sauce; and hot appetizers such as borek, or very thin pastry with various types of fillings and ciger mezesi, small cubes of liver with spring onions. Needless to say, this course is accompanied by the drink of the same name, raki, a spirit distilled from grapes or plums and flavoured with anise. At this point the meal would continue with what we would regard as the "first course," and which the Turkish people call the "yufka" course, comprising dishes such as puff pastry with a variety of fillings, or the famous pilaf rice, accompanied by the typical zeytinyagli (vegetables cooked in oil and served cold). The most famous of these has the colourful name of Imam Bayildi, "the Imam fainted." According to a rather charming legend the Imam (Muslim holy man) literally swooned with pleasure over a dish of aubergines and onions. Meat, particularly on formal occasions, is the focal point of a Turkish meal. Shish kebabs – the national dish based on cubes of lamb or mutton threaded on skewers and charcoal roasted – are now a familiar part of international cuisine.

Desserts and sweetmeats – the "luscious lips" and "lady's navels" – are very sweet indeed. They are made of flaky pastry, honey and nuts. The meal is rounded off with the traditional Turkish coffee.

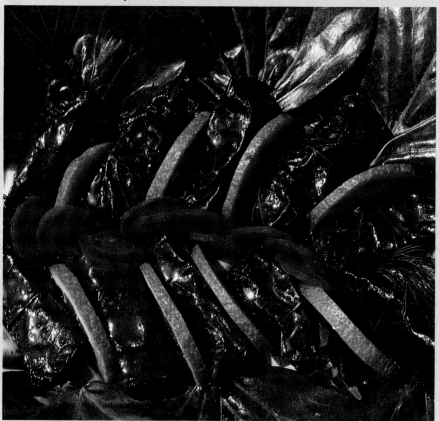

features. A few miles from the island of Gemile is a bay known as Ölü Deniz, or the "dead sea," a beautiful circular lagoon with bright blue water and beaches of very fine, white sand.

This is called the dead sea because it is practically a salt lake, with only a very narrow opening to the sea, preventing the normal exchange of water. For this reason, access to the bay has been prohibited to motorboats for some years now. To enter the bay, one must moor outside Ölü Deniz and row in. The effort will be rewarded by a magnificent view of this paradise, rescued at the eleventh hour from the potential hordes of boats and tourists.

From Ölü Deniz to Kalkan   33 nm

Let us head out to sea again, after enjoying the beauty of the bay of Ölü Deniz, for some hard sailing along a wild and inhospitable stretch of coastline known as the "Seven Capes." There are high mountains with sheer cliff walls, and it is hard to find shelter from the meltemi, which invariably blows from May to September throughout the eastern basin of the Mediterranean. In this area, it comes from the west. It batters the mountains and is channelled through deep gorges, gathering strength before striking the surface of the sea in powerful squalls. There are about 35 miles to Kalkan. A fresh wind and a sea with waves 1–1.5 m (3.3–5 ft) high make sailing strenuous, but at the same time exhilarating. In the late afternoon the barren mountains to port become tinged with warm colours. Before reaching the port of Kalkan, one sails past the ruins of Patara, clearly visible from the boat. However, it is not advisable to stop here as the wind can suddenly strengthen; it is better to stop at Kalkan, which has a safe harbour.

Once past the Seven Capes, the coast starts to level out, gradually rejoining the sea in a series of beaches. Kalkan lies in the broad gulf against a background of high mountains. The town is very attractive, and a perfect example of old Turkey: a beautiful mosque, a few shops and some quaint restaurants facing on to the harbour are the simple architectural features of this peaceful, unspoilt place. The harbour does not have a wall to moor along, but there is always room to anchor safely. This area is famous for two important archaeological sites: the ancient cities of Xanthos and Patara, 10 km (6 miles) from Kalkan.

On pages 88 and 89: a Lycian sarcophagus and a triple Roman arch at Patara – evidence of two different cultures which succeeded each other along this stretch of coast.

They can easily be reached by taxi or bus. Kalkan is still very much a place of traditional crafts and one can buy hand-made items, particularly clothes, which skilled tailors can produce in a few hours.

From Kalkan to Kaş   15 nm

Leaving Kalkan it is a short sail to the bay of Kaş, which is separated from the little Greek island of Kastellorizo by a strait barely 1.5 miles wide. The short distance means one can easily visit one of the most unspoiled places on the Mediterranean. It is worth stopping for a few hours at the picturesque harbour of Megisti, which is the only populated center on the island of Kastellorizo. There is no customs clearance at the harbour for entering and leaving Greek waters, but boats in transit are admitted provided they raise the courtesy flag. The island was of great strategic importance in the past, thanks

Below: a view of what is left of the once prosperous town of Kastellorizo. Badly damaged during the Second World War, its old houses are now gradually being restored (opposite) thanks to revenue from the tourist trade.

to its position in the lee of the Turkish coast, and the harbour was a busy trading port. This was the situation until the period of Italian rule ended in 1943, after which Kastellorizo, together with the Dodecanese archipelago, became Greek territory. It was somewhat neglected, mainly because of its considerable distance from Rhodes, the last Greek outpost before the Turkish coast. Part of the town is uninhabited today, but the peaceful atmosphere makes up for this decline, and this can be appreciated by walking along the harbour wall or by sampling the delicious fresh fish at one of the tavernas by the harbour.

The island also has some famous beauty spots. Not far from Megisti harbour, on the south-east coast, a little opening barely 1 m (3 ft) high leads to the wonderful blue grotto of Mavi Magara. To enter it, the sea must be perfectly calm, and one must use a little boat which can be hired at the harbour. The

ARCHAEOLOGY IN LYCIA

From Kalkan, one of the towns on our itinerary, it is a short ride by bus or taxi to the cities of Xanthos and Patara. They are about 10 km (6 miles) away and the journey takes one through little villages with all the atmosphere of old Turkey. These ancient cities played an important part in the development of civilization in Mediterranean Asia Minor. Xanthos was the capital of the Lycian League in the second century B.C., but the first settlements were built in the eighth century B.C. The city is situated on the banks of the Esen Cay river, which runs through it from north to south. It was ruled first by the Persians, then the Greeks and then the Romans. There is the famous square column at Xanthos standing 4 m (13 ft) high. The four sides are engraved with the longest piece of Lycian script to have survived and which has still not been fully translated. Passing through a gateway dating from the Hellenistic period, one enters the Roman acropolis. The Romans also built a large theater at Xanthos and an aqueduct which supplied water to the entire city. Three tombs from the Lycian period are to be found near the Roman theater: the finest is dedicated to the harpies, mythical creatures with the face of a woman and the body of an animal. It is mounted on a monolithic pyramid-shaped plinth. The city of Patara is 11 km (6.8 miles) from Xanthos and owes its importance to the flourishing trade which once passed through its port. The harbour basin eventually became silted up, turning it into a swamp. One building which gives an idea of how busy Patara was, is the huge granary built near the harbour at the time of Hadrian. The remains of the famous marble Vespasian baths which measured 105 × 48 m (344 × 157 ft) reflect the important role played by these cities in shaping an illustrious civilization.

grotto is about 60 m (200 ft) high inside and the only source of light is the narrow entrance. The light spreads over the surface of the water, reflecting on the walls, turning the grotto into a shimmering blue world. The grotto is inhabited by some Mediterranean seals, a species on the verge of extinction. If you are greeted by a loud roar on entering, it will be the seals protesting at the invasion of their home. They are usually stretched out on a rock at the back of the cave, and dive into the water the minute someone enters. It is a rare and moving experience to see these animals in their natural habitat. For this reason we should respect their environment, being careful not to drop litter or make too much noise. It is better to return to Turkish waters for the night, mooring in the friendly port of Kaş, the ancient Antiphellos.

This is a pretty little town and well supplied with shops and markets full of fruit and vegetables, where one can stock up on food. To the west of the town, near the sea, there is a small, perfectly preserved Greek theater dating from the Hellenistic period. Above Kaş stands a hill, where the ancient Lycians carved their tombs. These are still visible today, but

unlike the other tombs encountered on our route, these have been influenced by Persian art – further evidence of the rich cultural diversity of Turkey's history.

From Kaş to Gökkaya   18 nm

It is hard to work out exactly where the land ends and the sea begins. The Turkish coast between Kaş and Finike is a series of channels and deep bays which seem to be trying to confuse the sailor. Behind each cape, one comes across innumerable stretches of water at every point, in a continuous voyage of discovery. The island of Kekova a few miles from Kaş runs parallel to the coast. Sheltered inlets surrounded by luxuriant vegetation blend with the ruins of fortifications, the remains of cities buried by earthquakes, and Lycian sarcophagi, which are scattered all along this coast. On the northern side of the island of Kekova is the narrow strait of Tersane, about 100 m (330 ft) deep. This stretch of water contains some valuable relics including the partially-submerged ruins of a medieval Christian city and the apse of a fine Byzantine church. One can anchor in these bays

Above: an elegant veranda in the village of Kaş and, below, a view of the harbour.

and be not far from the beach which closes the gulf, and a short walk away from a well-preserved castle on the southern shore of the island.

On the coast, opposite Kekova, a narrow opening with two islets forms the entrance to the huge bay of Uçagiz (Turkish for "three openings"). There is no safer mooring in the whole of the Mediterranean. The water in the bay is very clean and its opaque colour is only due to the fact that there is a limited exchange with the open sea. Having moored in front of the village of Uçagiz, going ashore is like stepping into the past – one has a strong impression that nothing has changed here since the Middle Ages. There is no electricity and the dusty roads are mainly used by sheep and goats. However, it has the usual shoreline restaurants, which will provide a warm

Below: Lycian tombs on the coastline opposite the island of Kekova. Note the keel-shaped roofs of the sarcophagi. The Lycian people chose beautiful settings along the seashore for the eternal rest of their dead.

welcome and delicious food. As we sail eastwards, just before leaving the bay of Uçagiz, we pass the imposing medieval fortress built on the promontory of Kale Köy. Its strategic position dominates the entrance to the bay. Take care in mooring at Kale Köy as there are projecting sarcophagi and steps carved out of the rocks.

The village built on the slopes of the promontory climbs up as far as the fortress, its white houses standing out against the green palm and fig trees. There is a fine view from the top. The peaceful bay of Uçagiz stretches out to the right in contrast to the windy channel of the island of Kekova which winds round to the left. There is no end to the natural beauty of this coastline and before reaching Finike one really should stop in the bay of Gökkaya.

Overleaf: the amphitheater at Kale castle, which dominates the entrance to the bay of Uçagiz. From the buttresses of the citadel there is a superb view of the island of Kekova.

Above: the battlements of Kale castle look out over the island of Kekova, where small boats can moor at the picturesque anchorage of Tersane. The latter is dominated by the ruins of a church (below) which is probably of Byzantine origin.

This magnificent stretch of water is dotted with islands and rocks which provide wonderful moorings where one can enjoy a swim or even catch some of the numerous fish which live in these waters.

From Gökkaya to Çineviz Liman   35 nm

A visit to Finike, the ancient Phoenicus, provides a good excuse to stop at its small, well-equipped harbour and stock up on food before continuing up the Turkish coast. Splashes of colour brighten the coast around the town; orange trees thrive on the fertile plain and the very mild climate makes swimming possible all year round. Six km (3¾ miles) slightly inland from Finike is Limrya. A magnificent theater was built there in the fourth century which provided its spectators with shelter from bad weather by means of a huge cloth cover that was spread over the top steps. The history of this ancient city lives on through its countless ruins. A vast acropolis was built on the mountainside overlooking the city, containing many important tombs. One of the most outstanding is dedicated to Pericles, who made Limrya into the capital of the Lycian League in the fourth century B.C. and a stronghold of Greek resistance to Persian rule.

We head out to sea again rounding Cape Taslik, which closes the gulf of Finike with five little islands, and sailing back up the coast to Çineviz Liman. This broad bay is surrounded by mountains which are often covered in snow in winter. At Çineviz, a rich carpet of dense pine forests sweeps down to the sea. Stepping ashore is like stepping back into the Golden Age, into a landscape as yet untouched by man.

From Çineviz Liman to Antalya   29 nm

The last stretch of coast before Antalya presents a wealth of unusual features and places of outstanding natural beauty, guaranteed to provide you with happy memories of the Turkish coast. A large national park runs along the shore, starting at the ancient Olympos, immediately after Çineviz Liman. The ruins of Olympos are not visible from the sea, but it is worth stopping to visit them and then continuing eastwards for a few kilometers, as far as Chimera. Homer described this place as the home of a monster, part lion and part serpent, which breathed flames. The monster was killed by the Corinthian hero, Bellerophon, with the aid of the winged horse, Pegasus, and thereafter Chimera was destined to contain its fiery breath. The flames are in fact a spectacular geological phenomenon, particularly impressive at night, caused by gases (including methane) escaping from an underground pocket and igniting on contact with the air.

Traces of the past can be found all along this stretch of coast. Before mooring in Kemer harbour, the imposing ruins of ancient Phaselis can be seen on Tekirova peninsula. The most important civilizations have left their mark on this piece of land surrounded by sea and covered in vegetation: a Byzantine necropolis; a Roman aqueduct with its arches still intact; a Greek theater partly buried by undergrowth and two gateways which are now inaccessible, one at the north and the other at the south of the peninsula. These are the partly concealed treasures of Phaselis, which represent millennia of history. The city of Kemer has a brand new, very well-equipped marina, in one of the loveliest coastal settings in Turkey. An azure sea flanked by miles of white beach is enlivened by oleander, orange and lemon trees that exude a thoroughly Oriental flavour.

We follow the national park up the coast to Antalya, one of the liveliest and most interesting

THE ENVIRONS OF ANTALYA

For those who have time, there are some interesting excursions inland from Antalya. The important archaeological site of Termessos lies a few kilometers to the west. It commands an imposing position in the mountains and is full of monuments half buried by the dense vegetation. Near the village of Yacka, behind the eastern ridge, is Karain Cave. This is one of the largest caves in Anatolia, composed of three vast intercommunicating chambers. Excavations inside the cave have revealed that the first human settlements there date from the Lower Paleolithic Era. Since then thousands of people have used this natural refuge as a place of worship, or as a shelter. They have left a considerable amount of material in their wake, such as pointed fragments of bone, necklaces and tools for hunting and domestic use. Very near Antalya, to the east, there are two more important archaeological sites – the cities of Perge and Aspendos – both founded at the time of the conquest of Alexander the Great. To reach the beach at Lara, 12 km (7.4 miles) east of Antalya, one passes in front of the spectacular Düden Su Falls, in Düden Basi Park. They plunge over the sheer cliff straight into the sea. They are most impressive viewed from the boat.

towns in Turkey. There are cafés overlooking the harbour, which lies at the heart of the city, attractive restaurants along the palm-lined boulevard which runs from the top of the town to the sea, and parks that provide refuge from the midday heat. Antalya has a great deal to offer and it would be a shame to miss any of it. A good way to feel at home and to get to know the local people is to treat yourself to a Turkish bath, where you can enjoy a soothing massage at the hands of a skilled masseur.

To best appreciate the charm of Antalya, wander through the streets and discover the mosque of Alaedin Camil, the ancient Yivli minaret or the imposing Hadrian's arch. The archaeological museum, to the west of the city center, houses wonderful collections of ceramics and Lycian sarcophagi as well as some magnificent remains from ancient Zanthos. Many important cultural events also take place there in the summer.

The ruins of the ancient city of Phaselis on the Tekirova peninsula. This Greek amphitheater, now partly overgrown, reminds one of how important this stretch of coastline was in antiquity.

SARDINIA

Porto Cervo–La Maddalena archipelago–Santa Teresa di Gallura–Stintino–Alghero–Bosa–Torre Grande–Carloforte–Cagliari

Every sport has its paradise, and the coast of Sardinia is the ideal place for sailing. In many respects, it is the perfect natural environment, combining glorious colours and heady perfumes with a rugged coastline full of interesting places to discover. The history of this area is no less romantic, mariners and pirates having left traces of their exploits throughout the island. Sardinia was also inhabited in prehistoric times. These early civilizations were able to develop because they were protected from invasion by the winds which blow around the island; the shelters they built to shield themselves against the elements, known as nuraghi, indicate an advanced degree of sophistication.

The minute we leave Porto Cervo, on the north-east coast of the island, the mistral starts to blow. We head north towards the islands of La Maddalena archipelago, in the beautiful stretch of sea which separates Corsica from Sardinia. Returning to the Sardinian coast, we step ashore at Santa Teresa di Gallura, in the creek of Port Longone. Leaving the Straits of Bonifacio, we sail on round the northern coast into the gulf of Asinara. The coastline changes here, flattening out into beaches of golden sand. One can stop at the little town of Castelsardo before reaching Stintino at the western tip of the gulf of Asinara. At this point we leave the north coast of Sardinia to negotiate the Fornelli strait between the islands of Asinara and Piana, on the western side of Sardinia.

After reaching the wide natural harbour of Porto

One of the chief attractions of Sardinia is the wonderful colours of the coastline, every gulf, inlet and bay forming a beautiful picture. The sea, rocks and vegetation blend into a harmonious combination, and offer a true vision of paradise.

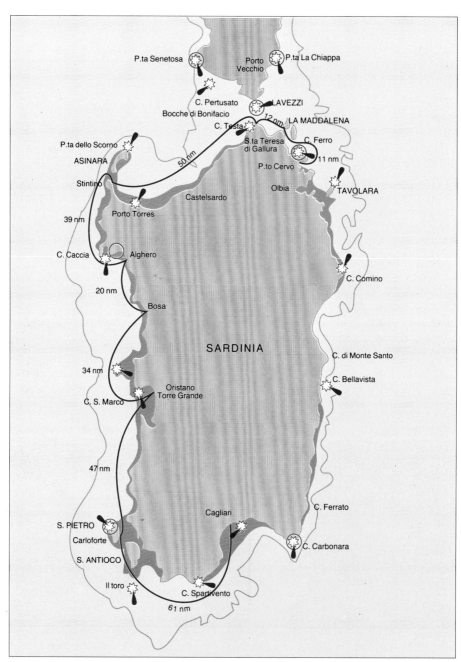

Distance covered: 274 nm.
Average temperatures: the average summer temperature on the coast is 28°C (82.4°F), rising to a maximum of 35–40°C (95°–104°F) in July and August.
Prevailing winds: the mistral often blows in the Straits of Boni-facio, at speeds of up to 35–40 knots, while the south-east of the island is affected by the sirocco.
Cartography: British Admiralty: 161A (Sardinia); 161B (Sardinia); 1212 (La Maddalena); 1204 (Porto Torres); 1202 (N. and W. coast ports); 1205 (Oristano); 1207 (Canale di San Pietro and Golfo di Palmas); 1211 (Capo Ferro to Capo Coda Cavallo).
Bibliography: Italian Waters Pilot (Imray Laurie Norie & Wilson); Corsica and Sardinia: A Visitor's Guide, Gerry Crawshaw (W. H. Allen).

Conte, we come to the town of Alghero. The coast is mountainous as far as Bosa Marina after which it becomes gentler, levelling out in the gulf of Oristano. Here, behind the beach, there is a fertile landscape, with lakes that are home to many birds and various animal species. This is another of the attractions of Sardinia: its environment and precious natural resources remain unharmed by man.

Having visited the ruins of Tharros at the north of the gulf of Oristano, we sail on past the sand dunes behind Cape Frasca, where the coast becomes hillier. We stop at Carloforte, a village on the island of San Pietro, a few miles from the Sardinian coast. There are usually only a few pleasure boats round the south-western part of Sardinia and this makes it one of the most unspoiled and enjoyable parts to visit. Having sailed round the west coast of the island of Sant'Antioco, we travel down towards Cape Teulada and round Cape Spartivento, the southern-most point of the island, then back up the coast to Cagliari, our final destination.

A strong breeze sweeps across the water, swelling the sails and showering the rocks with spray. Sardinia is a wonderful choice for a sailing holiday.

Porto Cervo – La Maddalena Archipelago   11 nm

The waters by the shoreline are emerald green, gradually turning bright blue and then a deeper blue the farther out one travels. This extraordinary sequence of colours is the hallmark of the Costa Smeralda (Emerald Coast), which extends along the north-eastern side of Sardinia. Our starting point is the fashionable tourist resort of Porto Cervo, which boasts one of the most attractive and best equipped marinas in the Mediterranean. If you are a keen party-goer and wish to get caught up in the social

The marina at Porto Cervo. This elegant and sophisticated resort is very much an international center for the smart sailing set. Opposite: a view of Porto Cervo.

whirl of the jet set, or even just admire the smartest yachts in the Mediterranean, then Porto Cervo is the place for you. The beauty of Porto Cervo is such that it inevitably attracts a large number of boats in summer. However, if you are lucky, you may find a quiet spot amid unspoiled scenery.

It is only a few miles from Porto Rotondo to the islands of La Maddalena archipelago, scattered across the windy Straits of Bonifacio. This is a wonderful place to explore by boat. After passing through the Biscie strait, one comes to the southern tip of the island of Caprera. These islands are sepa-

GARIBALDI: THE IMMORTAL LEGEND

Giuseppe Garibaldi, the Italian patriot and general who led the movement for the unification of Italy in the 1860s, was associated with Caprera for many years. On Caprera, a small island off the northern coast of Sardinia near La Maddalena archipelago, there is a harsh environment drenched in sunlight and sea spray and inhabited by unsophisticated, proud people. This place became the one stable factor in Garibaldi's life, a sanctuary where he could find strength and peace of mind before his missions. At his house, Casa Blanca, which is now open to the public, he was able to forget the turmoil of battle and retreat to the simple life. Caprera's granite coastline reflected the Spartan but generous nature of Garibaldi, who first came to the island in 1849. It was the scene of his great love affairs and finally also of his death. The history of Caprera and that of Garibaldi are thus inextricably entwined, a source of continued interest and inspiration to the visitor.

rated by beautiful stretches of water. Santo Stefano lies between the coast of Sardinia and the larger island of La Maddalena, which is so close to Caprera that it is linked to it by a bridge. Some say that God first created this idyllic group of islands and then used them as a model for paradise. Under the Kingdom of Savoy, they were known as the Intermediate Islands because of their location midway between Corsica and Sardinia. Because of this strategic position, they have long been the site of important naval bases. A visit to the Museum of Naval Archaeology is highly recommended. Situated on the east coast of La Maddalena island, it houses the remains of a Roman cargo ship.

La Maddalena Archipelago – Santa Teresa 12 nm

From La Maddalena archipelago, the Gallura region on the north coast of Sardinia is visible with the naked eye. We follow it westwards, leaving the island of Spargi to starboard and sailing back up to Punta Marmata. This stretch of coast is at its most magical at sunset, the soft light picking out the curious granite rocks of Cape Testa against the skyline, to the west of Santa Teresa. The wind and spray have eroded these rocks into bizarre shapes, making them look like giants sunning themselves on the shore after fierce battles with the sea. The harbour at Santa Teresa di Gallura brings us gently back to reality. One must be wary of rocks and sudden shoals along the coast

Cala Francese on the west coast of La Maddalena archipelago. This anchorage is very well sheltered and is still comparatively quiet, despite the ever increasing number of pleasure boats around the Sardinian coast.

Overleaf: a typical Sardinian seascape. Breakers driven by the west wind foam on the rocks below the Cape Orso lighthouse.

leading to Porto Longone, a deep creek open to the north and sheltered on either side by high cliffs. It forms a natural harbour for Santa Teresa and is sheltered from all but the mistral and west winds, which unfortunately cause an undertow. Santa Teresa used to be a famous center for red coral, and a few craftsmen keep the trade flourishing to this day. A visit to the town which lies on the promontory dominated by the massive, 41-m (135-ft) high Longosardo tower, provides an opportunity to stock up on food and enjoy a cool drink in the square.

Santa Teresa – Stintino   50 nm

Leaving Santa Teresa, we sail back past the granite rocks of Cape Testa, and the gulf of Asinara comes into view, opening out completely to the north. There are many anchorages along this coast, particularly near Isola Rossa, a barren island 400 m (1,300 ft) long, covered in bright red rocks, which runs very near to the coast.

Following the coast, which has no attractions in particular at this point, we arrive at Castelsardo, a little town built in a series of terraces on a promontory overlooking the sea.

We head towards Stintino on the opposite side of the gulf of Asinara, bypassing Porto Torres, which is

Overleaf: the ancient tower on the Pelosa beach at Stintino dominates the colourful waters of the Fornelli strait.

Below and opposite: the transparent waters of a rocky shoreline. In Sardinia there are many romantic spots like the one below, sometimes protected by ominous figures like the famous rock after which Capo Orso ("Bear Cape") is named (opposite). This rock was sculpted into this awesome shape by the wind.

of no great interest. Stintino is a picturesque fishing village built on a promontory with a long narrow inlet on either side of it, each of which has a small harbour. The southernmost is Porto Minore, which is reserved for fishing vessels with a maximum draft of a couple of meters; the other is Porto Mannu, where some pontoons have been provided for pleasure boats.

This village has an unusual history. It was built in 1896 to house the inhabitants of the island of Asinara, who were evacuated after a penal colony was built there. Asinara itself is a few miles to the north and landing there is strictly forbidden. Sailing through the area between Asinara and Isola Piana which lies between it and the coast, known as the Fornelli Strait, you will see some of the loveliest scenery in Sardinia.

The water in the Fornelli Strait is very shallow, varying from 2–5 m (6–16 ft), but the colour of the water, taking on countless different shades of turquoise with every variation in depth of the seabed, will more than make up for any difficulty of navigation. The infinite variety of this single colour provides a rich visual contrast to the barren islands on either side of the strait.

Sardinia is world famous for its translucent waters and, weather permitting, it is worth stopping for a swim in one of the little bays at the south of Isola Piana before tackling the strait, and sailing down the western side of the island.

Stintino – Alghero   39 nm

Having rounded Cape Falcone, we sail in a southerly direction down the western side of Sardinia, coasting the peninsula which separates us from the gulf of Asinara. This is one of the most attractive areas for sailing in the whole of the Mediterranean. Almost certainly aided by a north wind, the tail-end of the mistral, we follow a craggy coastline broken up here and there by dazzling beaches offset by white cliffs. It is tempting to stop at every picturesque cove, but it would take months to explore this coast fully.

The flight of a cormorant between the projecting rocks tells us that we are approaching Cape Caccia, a limestone promontory. Erosion by wind and sea has sculpted the rock into wonderful shapes both above and below sea level, in an endless sequence of caves and gorges. There are dozens of grottoes along the

CASTELSARDO

The little town of Castelsardo (illustrated on pages 116–117) was founded in the twelfth century by the Genoese, who named it Castel Genovese. It subsequently came under Spanish domination and was renamed Castel Aragonese. The present name was given to it in 1720 when it passed to the Kingdom of Piedmont, together with the rest of the island. The town is dominated by the Cathedral of Sant'Antonio Abate, built on the cliff edge. It has some fine paintings by an unknown sixteenth-century artist known as the Master of Castelsardo, and a grey trachyte bell tower with a majolica-covered dome. From the cathedral there is a clear view of the gulf of Asinara, with the mountains of Corsica in the background. The combination of the grey cathedral walls, the sapphire blue sea and the dark shadows of the distant Corsican mountains form a memorable picture. Castelsardo still has a thriving craft industry, producing unusual baskets made from the leaves of wild palm trees that grow along the shore. They are decorated with figures of deer, birds and other motifs, set against an ivory-coloured background.

west side of the coast of Cape Caccia including Neptune's Grotto, the mythical scene of the sea god's trysts with the nymphs, which is covered in stalagmites that are up to 6 m (20 ft) in diameter. As one cannot moor near the entrance to the cave, the best thing is to drop anchor in Porto Conte bay, which reaches inland for nearly 5 km (3 miles). Porto Conte, with its many pretty coves, is a paradise for swimmers. The innermost part of the bay looks almost like a lagoon, with shallow water extending for about 90 m (300 ft) from the shore. Enjoy the changing colour effects created by the play of light on the rocks at dusk, and spend a peaceful night here. In the morning, refresh yourself with a relaxing swim in the glassy, emerald green water.

Immediately after leaving Porto Conte, we come to Alghero, one of the most interesting towns in Sardinia. Founded by the Genoese in the twelfth century, it soon came under Spanish rule. The Spaniards established a Catalan settlement here and the local dialect still shows strong traces of Catalan.

To stop at Alghero harbour, one has to berth at the customs wharf, where fuel and water are available. The fortifications surrounding the town were built in the sixteenth century and are an interesting example of the degree of technical skill which the main towns along the coast achieved in their efforts to defend themselves against enemies and pirates. Two days not to be missed are 26 and 27 August, when a lateen-sail regatta is held.

SARDINIAN CUISINE

Authentic Sardinian cuisine has extremely ancient roots, and its traditions are kept very much alive in home cooking to this day.

It is a basic, frugal type of cuisine, originally influenced by poverty and the austere life led by the islanders. The shepherds of Barbagia existed for months on a diet of "pane carasau," known as "sheet music," crisp paper-thin sheets of bread that have to be softened in boiling water prior to eating. Dishes are flavoured with herbs, but never spicy. They are based on roast lamb and the famous "porceddu" (suckling pig, illustrated), offal (entrails), game (mainly songbirds, such as blackbirds and thrushes, known as "pillonis de taccula"), bread, dairy produce, honey and dried pulses. Out of this tradition, famous specialities have emerged, such as "maloreddus," (a type of gnocchi), "sa fregula," (semolina balls in broth), "culigionis," (cheese and potato ravioli), "sebadas," (fresh cheese and honey fritters) and the delicious caciofiore (a cheese made from ewe's milk).

Fish dishes are a more recent addition to this culinary tradition, although still a few hundred years old. They are the legacy of the foreign sailors, navigators and pirates from Spain, Genoa, Tuscany and Sicily, who settled on the Sardinian coast.

Recipes showing these foreign influences include "cassola" (a stew made of at least twelve different types of fish), "sa burrida" (dogfish with walnut sauce, eaten as an appetizer), and various recipes for swordfish and lobster. "Su mazzamurru" (stale bread soup) is another import, and was at one time the staple diet of galley slaves. Eel and mullet are caught along the coast and in lakes and two very unusual dishes are prepared from the latter. These are "merca," in which the fish is boiled in salt water and wrapped in reeds to preserve it, and "bottariga," mullet (sometimes tuna fish) roes, which are salted and dried then served with tomato salad or pasta.

Sardinian sweets are nearly always made with almonds. The wines are excellent and include Cannonau, Vermentino, Monica, Torbato, Vernaccia and Malvasia.

Alghero–Bosa   20 nm

At this point we can enjoy a thoroughly good sail
along the west coast of Sardinia, which becomes
increasingly ripply after Alghero, sloping down in
terraces to the sea. The sea is, as always, the most
important feature of our journey – endlessly absorb-
ing and at the same time thoroughly relaxing. Having
followed a coast of white rocks covered in vivid green
Euphorbia arborea, we reach Bosa Marina. This
harbour, connected to the ancient town of Bosa by a
bridge over the mouth of the river Temo, is a very
comfortable spot to moor in, being protected by a
causeway which joins the little Isola Rossa to the
coast. The crowded harbours of the Costa Smeralda
are a distant memory here. The little town of Bosa
is dominated by the twelfth-century castle on
Serravalle hill, which was built by the Malaspina
family and has a commanding view of the Temo
valley.

The Temo is the only navigable river in Sardinia. It
is worth travelling a short way up it in the tender, to
visit the Sas Conzas, the old tanneries which remained in operation until the end of the nineteenth
century. Continuing upstream a little, past banks
covered in fruit and olive trees, we come to the
picturesque church of San Pietro Extramuros. It was
built in stages between 1000 and 1300, using different
architectural styles, the main body of the church
being Romanesque and the side aisles Gothic.

Bosa–Torre Grande   34 nm

We now set off to discover a part of Sardinia which is
quite different to the places we have visited so far.
After leaving Bosa Marina, the coast begins to
soften, and by the time one is in sight of Cape
Mannu, it is completely flat. At this point we are
sailing along the Sinis peninsula, opposite Mal di
Ventre island, the south side of which provides a safe
mooring in fair weather. It is a good excuse to stop
and enjoy an unspoiled environment, surrounded by
clean water where fish live in abundance. After passing Cape San Marco, we enter the broad gulf of
Oristano. This is encircled by the most fertile plain in
Sardinia, a vast area coloured by fruit trees and pine
and eucalyptus woods.

The most picturesque mooring is at Marina di

On pages 120 and 121: the smooth surface of a calm sea acts as a perfect foil to the striking geometrical rock formations at Cape Caccia.

Below: the houses at Bosa Marina on a hot summer's day. The boats are reflected in the peaceful waters of the river Temo, the only navigable river in Sardinia. The mouth of the river is shown in the picture opposite, top right.

Torre Grande, between Is Barracas and the large octagonal tower built by the Spanish in the seventeenth century at the north of the gulf of Oristano. There are some good anchorages before the Circolo di Oristano, near the mouth of the canal leading to the great Cabras pool, a shallow lake a little way inland. Fishermen use the pool to shelter from southerly winds, and its calm waters are home to many species of waterfowl. However, it is really only possible to sail up into it if one is familiar with the shallows at the entrance to the canal.

The gulf of Oristano has one of the most interesting archaeological sites in Sardinia. This consists

of the ruins of Tharros at the base of the narrow peninsula of San Giovanni di Sinis, which ends with Cape San Marco. Tharros has a fascinating history. The Phoenicians built a village here over the ruins of earlier buildings. It then became Carthaginian and subsequently Roman, together with the rest of Sardinia. There are traces of Byzantine culture up to the year 1000, after which the village of Tharros came to be abandoned and lay covered with sand until the nineteenth century, when it was ransacked by thieves. Serious excavations of the area began in the mid twentieth century, when evidence of many centuries of Sardinian history was unearthed.

CARLOFORTE, A LIGURIAN ENCLAVE

In the sixteenth century, a group of people from Pegli, a village near Genoa, left their native region of Liguria and set sail for Tabarca, a little island 170 km (105 miles) from the Tunisian coast, to trade in coral.

Following the Saracen invasions in the early eighteenth century, the inhabitants of Tabarca, including the Genoese settlers, had to flee the island and sought refuge on San Pietro Island, at the invitation of the King of Savoy, Carlo Emanuele III.

As a gesture of gratitude to the king for allowing them to establish another town in which to trade in fishing, the refugees from Tabarca built a

statue of him (illustrated below) which can be seen near the harbour. Since then, Carloforte has kept the Genoese traditions alive through each generation resisting, with characteristic Ligurian tenacity, conquest first by the French and then by the Spanish.

Because of this historical connection, the people of Carloforte speak a dialect which is quite different from Sardinian, and is more akin to the Genoese dialect. The bright colours with which their boats, doors and windows are painted are also typical features of Liguria and its traditions.

GIARA DI GESTURI

The best and most enjoyable way in which to survey the natural beauties of Sardinia is on horseback.

Viewing the world from this vantage point, as the Sardinian shepherds would, helps the visitor to gain a better understanding of what it is like to live in an unspoiled environment, such as that of the Giara of Gesturi – a 12-km (7½-mile) plateau inland from Oristano. Here, in a cork oak wood or near the dried-up ponds, one could well come across a herd of the famous wild horses of Gesturi, a small breed imported by the Phoenicians about

3,000 years ago. About the same size as ponies, their bodies are perfectly proportioned, and they live in groups of up to 50 animals. They are the ultimate expression of a wild and as yet unspoiled countryside.

Many other animal species live undisturbed in the Giara di Gesturi, including boar, hare and partridge. As one learns more about this world, one can appreciate how easy it is to destroy the works of nature and at the same time how impossible it is for mankind to achieve such harmonious perfection.

THE NURAGHI

The plains around the gulf of Oristano reveal many traces of an ancient civilization which developed between 1500 and 1000 B.C., and which, it now seems certain, had its origins in Greece. Ancient Greek historians attributed the distinctive architecture of the nuraghi to Daedalus, the foremost architect in Greek mythology. Their buildings look a bit like sand castles, being shaped like upturned buckets. One of the best preserved nuraghi sites is the village of Su Nuraxi at Barumini (below) in the Gesturi plain. It consists of a close network of flattened conical buildings, which were used as dwellings, dominated by the large nuraghe of Santu Antine built at the top of a hill. The village was clearly a powerful stronghold and shows how proficient these people were at building massive stone structures. This nuraghe has defied wind, rain and the intense summer heat for nearly 26 centuries. It is commonly believed that the nuraghi were built to defend the island's inhabitants from enemy forces. However, the fact that they are distributed fairly uniformly throughout the island suggests that this was not the case, and that they were proof of clan ownership of a given territory – a symbol of power which became increasingly well-organized and complex over the course of time. Isolated nuraghi thus came to be replaced by complete fortified villages like the one at Barumini, which is similar in many respects to a medieval fortification with a castle protected by towers and covered passages.

Very little is in fact known about this civilization, although all the evidence, from the bronze statuettes to the communal graves known as the "giants' tombs," suggests that its craftsmen were highly skilled. The nuraghi were abandoned in about the ninth century B.C., although the civilization surrounding them endured for longer, changing its customs and types of dwelling. At about that time, the first Phoenician merchants landed on Sardinia and they may have succeeded the Mycenaeans in trading with the coastal areas of Sardinia. It was probably the Phoenicians who introduced the art of bronze-working. All these different peoples brought their own cultures with them, gradually altering the customs of the Sardinians and enriching life there in a way that was matched by few other countries in antiquity.

Torre Grande – Carloforte   47 nm

On page 131: two surviving Roman columns from the ruins of the city of Nora set against the coastline at Cape Pula.

The voyage continues along an unusual stretch of the Sardinian coastline. Having left the anchorage at Torre Grande, we head for Cape Frasca on the other side of the gulf of Oristano, past distant, sun-soaked beaches. A word of warning: military exercises are sometimes carried out around this cape, with low-flying jet aircraft firing at targets on the coast. If these are in evidence, it is best to head out to sea. The coast is covered with sand-dunes shaped by the wind and surrounded by hills with a dense cover of rosemary and myrtle. These different shades of green form a wonderful contrast with the deep tones of the sea. We follow a continuous line of sandhills for miles, reminiscent of the coast of North Africa. Having rounded Cape Pecora, the scenery changes, bays of white sand alternating with jagged cliffs splintered and strewn over a green sea. This was a mining area at the beginning of the twentieth century, and the remains of the mining villages can be seen near the natural harbour of Buggerru.

After sailing past high cliffs, we reach the island of

Below: the fishermen still build reed huts around the Cabras pool, using age-old techniques. One of Sardinia's main attractions is that it retains many such traditions.

RETRACING THE ISLAND'S HISTORY

It was the Phoenicians who first recognized the commercial importance of Sardinia. They were a race of merchants and navigators who established ports of call on the island in the process of expansion towards the Iberian peninsula. These soon became colonies.

Nora was the first Phoenician settlement on Sardinia. It grew up near the town of Pula, at the westernmost point of the gulf of Cagliari. It is surrounded by sea and has many ruins dating from the earliest days of Sardinia's history, through years of conquest, changes of leadership and contact with different cultures. After the Phoenicians, Nora was conquered by the Carthaginians and then the Romans. Columns, an amphitheater, the remains of a Carthaginian temple dedicated to the goddess Tanit and fine Roman Baths testify to this city's varied history. Our search for traces of the first foreign settlements in Sardinia continues south. Just before Cape Spartivento we come across the Punic-Roman ruins of Bithia, consisting of a vast necropolis and sanctuaries dominated by the seventeenth-century Chia tower. The trail leads to the island of Sant'Antioco in the Sulcis archipelago, where numerous "tophets" of Carthaginian origin are to be found in the town of the same name. These were circles with an altar at the center on which children were sacrificed to the gods.

The sea has played an important part in the civilization of mankind, bringing to the shores of Sardinia a succession of different cultures.

San Pietro and step ashore at Carloforte, one of the most interesting resorts in Sardinia. Carloforte, where the air is thick with the fragrance of basil, is a town of narrow streets climbing up a hillside between brightly painted houses. Tempting aromas waft throughout this little town: at mealtimes, the narrow streets exude the perfume of freshly prepared pesto sauce and grilled fish. Try some of the local seafood specialities, such as gilthead, mullet and lobster. Although Carloforte gave up tuna fishing years ago, the fishermen of the island of San Pietro still ensure a regular supply of other fresh fish. The southern part of the island of San Pietro is particularly attractive, with high cliff walls full of narrow inlets and bays such as Spalmatore bay, for example, to the south-east where you can admire the manifold treasures of the seabed through the clear waters.

Carloforte – Cagliari   61 nm

The islands of San Pietro and Sant'Antioco form the Sulcis archipelago, named after one of the oldest Phoenician settlements in Sardinia. After leaving Carloforte, we head south through the San Pietro channel and then coast the western side of the island of Sant'Antioco. South-western Sardinia has a wild, inhospitable shore with sparse vegetation, but this starkness is one of its attractions. The harsh environment is mirrored in the furrowed, weathered faces of the Sardinian shepherds.

Having reached Cape Sperone at the southern tip of Sant'Antioco, the gulf of Palmas opens out to the left, at the interior of which is Ponte Romano, named after a bridge built in Roman times which is visible near the harbour walls. This harbour links Sant'Antioco to the mainland, from which it is separated by a causeway. There are many peaceful bays in the gulf, with very few tourists. However, if one is pressed for time, it is better to stop at Porto Malfatano beyond the gulf of Teulada. This is another area where military exercises are carried out. These take place throughout the year, except in August, and one should be very wary of low-flying jets firing at targets on dry land. If you hear the sound of their engines, your best course is to head out to sea as far away as possible from Cape Teulada. At Porto Malfatano is the little island of Tauredda, which has the most picturesque moorings along this stretch of coast, in a

The Spanish tower at Canai point on the southern part of the island of Sant'Antioco. Below it, the sea changes colour from emerald green to deep blue within the space of a few yards.

setting of pine woods and bright blue sea. At the eastern tip of Porto Malfatano is Cape Spartivento, with shallow waters and a dangerous shoal 3.5 (11 ft 6 in) below water, 450 m (1,500 ft) to the south. After the cape, we start back up the coast of Sardinia to Cape Pula, a conical promontory surmounted by a Spanish tower. At Cape Pula one can moor near the ruins of the city of Nora, a Phoenician port discovered in the 1950s, with a colonnaded Roman theater facing on to the sea, which looks very peace-

ful at sunset. We continue our journey into the gulf of
Cagliari and up to Cagliari itself, the capital of Sardinia. Behind the city are two salt lakes inhabited by
herons and cormorants – a final glimpse of a natural
scene which makes a pleasing end to our journey.

Long, deserted white sand beaches wait to be admired behind every headland.

On pages 136 and 137: the waters of Sardinia are perfect for sailing.

FRANCE

CORSICA

St. Florent–Calvi–Girolata–Propriano–Bonifacio
Porto Vecchio

Corsica is a world in itself: a mountain rising from the sea. It lies in the heart of the western Mediterranean, cradled between the French and Italian coasts, which seem both so accessible yet remote. Every aspect of the island is worth exploring: its geology, history, flora and fauna; the beauty of its coastline, forests and mountains; its gentle and violent aspects. Furthermore, this extraordinary variety of landscape is to be found in a relatively small area.

Corsica is the fourth largest island in the Mediterranean. The west side of the island has an irregular coastline, with countless places to explore. Having a crystalline geological structure, mainly composed of granite, porphyry, gneiss and granulite, the west coast is craggy and broken up into promontories and deep gulfs, in a spectacular range of colours ranging from red to ocher and pink to grey. These provide sheltered inlets and beautiful bays which are inaccessible from the mainland. At the same time, one only has to explore a short way inland to come across alpine scenery with high mountains (Mount Cinto is 2,710 m [8,890 ft] high) covered in dense forests with rare trees such as Corsican pines. The intense green is broken by the crystal waters of rivers and torrents. Villages perch on the sides of mountains or on terraces. Built from local stone, they almost seem a natural part of the landscape. Meeting the islanders will make your visit all the more enjoyable. They are an unsophisticated, warm and hospitable people, of ancient Italic origin.

Let us therefore set sail without further ado, and explore this extraordinary miniature continent. We will concentrate on the west coast, which is the most interesting, with a few short trips inland.

Aerial view of the town and watch-tower of Porto, situated at the end of the gulf of the same name. The entire west coast of Corsica is punctuated by broad bays and narrow inlets, all providing delightful refuge from the mistral blowing hard from the north-west.

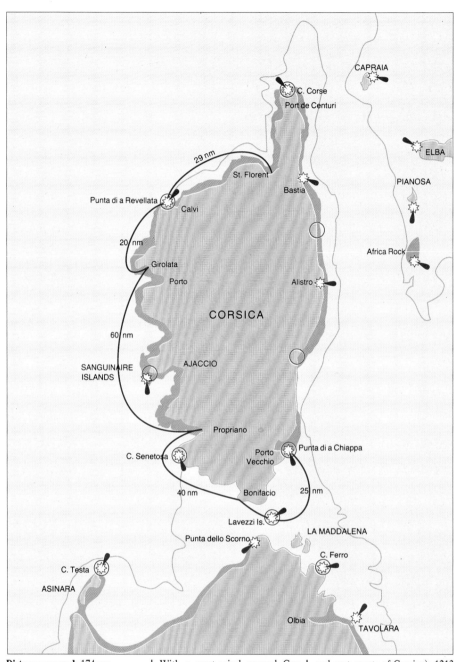

Distance covered: 174 nm.
Average temperatures: Cap Corse 16.6°C (65°F); Ajaccio 14.7°C (59°F); Bonifacio 15.7°C (62°F); 24°C (74°F) in summer.
Prevailing winds: in summer on the west coast, north-west to south-west winds, up to force 6.

With a west wind around Cap Corse, violent squalls.
Cartography: British Admiralty: 1992 (Parts of Sardinia and Corsica with Bonifacio Strait); 1131 (Island of Corsica); 1424 (Ports on the south and west coasts of Corsica); 1425 (Ports on the north

and east coasts of Corsica); 1213 (Bonifacio Strait).
Bibliography: Blue Guide to Corsica (A. & C. Black, London. W. W. Norton, New York); Instructions Nautiques Corse (S.H.O.M. – in French).

Beware of winds and the weather. The prevailing winds are westerlies, which tend to come from the north-west and veer south-west. These can be very strong on occasion, so it is not wise to rely on anchorages except for short stops for a swim. It is best to find sheltered inlets for the night.

We begin our cruise at the delightful town of St. Florent, situated in the gulf of the same name, at the base of the "finger" at the north of Corsica. About 30 miles' sailing takes us to Calvi along a wild, irregular coastline where rocky areas alternate with white sandy beaches and with interesting places at which to stop if the weather is good. Calvi is a lively, pictur-esque town, dominated by a Genoese fortress and with a well sheltered harbour. The second stage of our journey, from Calvi to Girolata along a much steeper, rockier coastline, is shorter (20 miles). This gives us time to appreciate some of the most spec-

Inside the fjord leading to Bonifacio there are steep-sided rocky inlets which, being uninhabited, are much quieter anchorages than the harbour at Bonifacio, usually overcrowded with yachts and ferries.

tacular scenery in Corsica. The colours of the sea-scapes at Elbo and Girolata are breathtaking. The third stage, from Girolata to Propriano (60 miles) is less wild and not as stunning. However, those who are interested in history can stop off at Ajaccio, the birthplace of Napoleon. There is also the archaeological site of Filitosa, which can be reached from Porto Pollo, on the north coast of the Gulf of Valinco. The fourth stage of our journey, from Propriano to Bonifacio (40 miles), skirts a coastline of pink granite

The little lighthouse on Punta della Madonetta marks the entrance to Bonifacio fjord. This part of the coast has high cliffs which are recognizable from afar.

framed by the green of the Mediterranean maquis. There are numerous rocks offshore and plenty of possible anchorages. The coast bends southeastwards and the deep bay of Figari, inaccessible from the mainland, provides a safe haven before reaching the town of Bonifacio. Set high on cliffs of white limestone, it dominates the notorious Straits of Bonifacio, where the channelled winds are strengthened by at least two points. Crossing the straits calls for all one's skill as a sailor, but greatly adds to the

excitement of a cruise. Afterwards, one can relax on the final stage, from Bonifacio to Porto Vecchio. The coast becomes much softer and greener after the strait, with a succession of broad, welcoming bays such as Santa Manza and Rondinara.

From St. Florent to Calvi   29 nm

Our journey begins at St. Florent, situated at the north of the gulf of St. Florent and at the mouth of the river Aliso. The river flows along the Nebbio basin, of which St. Florent is the main center. The town has a troubled history, having been ravaged by malaria and long fought over by the French and Genoese. Thanks to the growth of the water-sports industry, it has now become a very well-equipped tourist port. Before setting sail, it is worth strolling through the narrow, winding streets of the old town, pausing at one of the little cafés and then continuing as far as the Genoese citadel, where there is a fine

St. Florent has a modern, well-equipped marina protected by the old town, whose Genoese-style houses are tinged with the golden late-afternoon sun.

view of the old town. If you are so inclined, you could hire a car and explore the Nebbio basin – named after the fog ("nebbia" in Italian) which descends there when the mistral blows – and try some of the famous Vermentino wine which is produced there. The church of Santa Maria Assunta 1 km (⅔ mile) from the center is also worth visiting. Built in a simple Pisan-Romanesque style, with Corsican decoration, it contains the remains of Saint Flor.

To reach Calvi, we will have to cross the gulf of St. Florent and follow the rugged coast of the Désert des Agriates. This is one of the most unspoiled parts of the island as it is virtually inaccessible by land. In spring, it is coloured pink and mauve by a profusion of anemones and wild sage. If the weather is really fine you could stop opposite the long, white beach at Saleccia, set against a backdrop of green shrubs and pine trees. In the distance stand the peaks of the Désert des Agriates. Ipana is the highest peak at 478 m (1,568 ft).

CAP CORSE

From St. Florent, a trip to Cap Corse, known in ancient times as "the sacred promontory," enables one to fit another piece into the vivid mosaic of Corsica. This is an area of contrasting colours; rocks and cliffs are vivid green and black, as are the roofs of the houses. The coast between Cap Corse and Île de la Giraglia is dark and harsh, a forbidding stretch of land that exerts its own particular fascination. It is about 20 miles from St. Florent to the other side of Cape Grosso at the far north of Corsica. The little uninhabited island of Giraglia stands guard over the area, with its powerful light. Each July the boats of the famous Toulon-Giraglia regatta sail past. One can stop opposite it in the deserted bay of Barcag-gio, which is exposed to winds from the open sea. Hewn from the green and black rocks, the bay is bordered to the east by a long beach where one can anchor. Weather permitting, the peaceful little fishing port of Centuri (below), a few miles south of Cape Grosso, is a good place to stop for the night on the way back to St. Florent. One can sample the local lobster at one of the little restaurants and reflect on the history of Cap Corse and its hard-working people, who have always been more closely linked with the sea than the inhabitants of the rest of the island. Rejected by a harsh and hostile land, they sought and achieved prosperity through fishing, trade and voyages to distant lands.

Watch out for the small shoals at Punta di Curza. Alternatively, after about three miles, Malfalco bay offers good shelter, especially with a moderate westerly. Although the beautiful pine wood has been destroyed by fire, an interesting botanical reserve has been established there. The coast becomes progressively less wild and more populated with stretches of sand alternating with rocky patches. A road runs close to the shoreline and the land is farmed.

Ten miles from Malfalco, Île Rousse provides the only safe shelter in bad weather. The harbour has no special features, but there is an interesting village a short walk away. At the heart of the village is Paoli Square, where people play "petanque" (a game similar to bowls). It is shaded by plane and palm trees and has a fountain in the center with a bust of Paoli, under whom Corsica briefly became an independent nation.

Overleaf and on page 151: there are many good beaches south of Porto, with deep blue water offset by red cliffs.

Below: the massive plinth of the citadel of Calvi dominates the gulf and harbour below, which are sheltered from the mistral. After a hard day's sailing, an excursion to the citadel provides a chance to relax and enjoy its panoramic views.

It is best not to dawdle after Île Rousse, but head straight for Calvi. Watch out for the dangerous Algajola shoal just 80 cm (2 ft 6 in) below water. The shoal is not clearly marked with danger warnings, but it lies a mile from the coast, north-west of the town of Algajola. If the mistral has started to blow, Calvi will provide a welcome opportunity to relax. Leaving the boat protected by the rocky peninsula on which the Genoese citadel stands, one can take a leisurely look at one of the most interesting towns in Corsica, before preparing for a long stretch along a spectacular piece of coastline.

From Calvi to Girolata   20 nm

"Civitas Calvi semper fidelis" (The ever loyal city of Calvi). These words are carved over the gateway to the citadel which was built by the Genoese at the end of the fifteenth century. Because of its strategic and commercial importance, Calvi was bitterly contested in the past, but as these words testify, it was loyal to Genoa and later to France. In any case, Calvi was more attached to the mainland than to the rest of the island. It is the capital of La Balagne, one of the most fertile regions on the island, abounding in orchards and market gardens. The half-ruined citadel and fortifications deserve a thorough visit. They command a superb view of the bay with its myriad shades of blue. The church of St John the Baptist and the chapel of the brotherhood of St Anthony are not to be missed. Heading back down towards the harbour, we retrace our steps along the Promenade des Pêcheurs as far as the Tour du Sel, where salt was once stored. We leave behind the busy cafés and little restaurants, past the Hôtel de Ville (Town Hall), and venture as far as the cemetery, where there are good views of the citadel and bay.

If there is enough time, it would be a pity to miss the forest of Bonifato which is about 20 km (12.4 miles) inland. The Figarella river cuts through the forest which has over 3,000 hectares (7,413 acres) of pinasters (cluster pines), chestnut trees, holm oaks and Corsican pines. You can also visit the famous Bonifato "circle": a natural amphitheater formed from granite rocks. There are some lovely walks in the area and one can bathe in the natural rock pools of the Figarella river.

Before leaving Calvi you should stock up with the

CORSICAN CUISINE

Many aspects of the original Corsican culinary tradition have now disappeared, particularly the old stone pots and ovens, and the use of chestnut flour as the basis for a range of recipes such as "fanculelle" (sweets cooked in chestnut leaves and filled with cheese), polenta, fritters, "nicci, brilluli, torta castagnina" (cakes) and so forth. Chestnut woods abound in Corsica, and chestnuts feature greatly in its cuisine. However, there are plenty of other specialities to satisfy the curiosity and appetite of those looking for the authentic flavours and recipes of Corsica. There are also many dishes cooked in olive oil, which was once produced at the many presses along the banks of rivers and streams.

First courses include delicious vegetable and red bean stews, ravioli, lasagna and Bouillabaisse, a fish soup served with garlic croûtons, known here as "aziminu." The cured pork (illustrated) is particularly flavoursome, made from half-wild pigs which are crossed with wild boar and smoked using aromatic herbs from the maquis. Cuts include "coppa," veined with fat, "lonzu," lean fillet, and "prisuttu" and "figatelli," which are smoked sausages made from heart, liver and kidneys. Fish dishes include fresh lobster, available all along the coast, and freshwater trout. There are also fish stews, fried fish, grilled mullet and sardines. Meat dishes include delicious cutlets of lamb and kid roasted with herbs, tripe and onions, stewed pork and Andouillettes de Bonifacio (lamb chitterlings).

Cheeses include "brocciu" (a delicious fresh ewe's or goat's cheese which is included in many sweet and savoury recipes) and mature cheeses like the sharp-tasting "niolo." Sweets include "fiadone" (a tart flavoured with orange-flower water), "canistrelli" (made from almonds and hazelnuts and flavoured with aniseed), candied citrons, fruit jellies and aromatic honey.

There are plenty of good Corsican wines, the industry having recently been actively promoted and strictly regulated. In 1972, standards were laid down for Corsican wines. They include Patrimonio, which is available in red, white and rosé, Côteaux de Cap Corse in the north, and Porto Vecchio and Figari Pianottoli in the south. Wine-tasting is often possible in the areas where it is produced. Grape varieties include Nielluccio and Sciacarello (red wine) and Vermentino and Muscat (white wine).

delicious local food. It would also be as wise to make sure that the weather forecast is stable before leaving, so that no worries will mar your enjoyment of this wonderful stretch of coast.

If the sea is calm, one can moor in front of the Grotte des Veaux Marines (a grotto where Mediterranean seals used to be found) between Punta di a Revellata and Cape Cavallo (8 km/5 miles). The ravine of Porto Agro and the bay of Nichiaretto are two deserted spots set against a wonderful backdrop of scenery. After Cape Cavallo and Cape Morsetta, one can bypass the anchorages of Crovani bay and the gulf of Galeria, where the Fango valley cuts through the mountains. These are only accessible in fine weather. From here to Girolata, the coast becomes inaccessible from the mainland, and after the beautiful, completely wild bay of Focolara, the 560-m (1,837-ft) high Scandola peninsula rises up between Punta Palazzo and Punta Rossa. It is a nature reserve protected by strict legislation. Here one finds precipitous rocks, porphyries eroded into countless different shapes, rare plants like *armenia solenocii*, marine flora such as diatoms and posidoniae. The fauna includes marsh harriers, eagles and cormorants, and fascinating underwater creatures such as corals and lobsters. Unfortunately the monk seal, which used to live in this area, disappeared some time ago. After Focolara bay, Elbo marina provides one of the most spectacularly beautiful anchorages in Corsica. This breathtaking narrow inlet contrasts the reddest rocks with the bluest water and greenest vegetation imaginable. Note that one cannot stay longer than 24 hours here. This regulation is designed to protect the park and its wildlife.

Continuing on our way, providing the weather is still good, one can pass between the islet and Punta Palazzo and, very carefully, between the little island of Gargalo and the coast. The cliffs are red here too, and the sea is inky blue. On the island, home to countless birds which must not be disturbed, stand a Genoese watch-tower and a lighthouse. Rounding the promontory of Punta Rossa, we finally enter the grandiose gulf of Girolata, with a transparent blue sea, surrounded by cliffs of red and violet porphyry. The air is full of the fragrance of eucalyptus trees. There is a wonderfully peaceful atmosphere, due to the absence of cars, although in high season this is spoilt by the engine noise of dinghies.

On pages 152 and 153: the watch-tower of Porto is built on a rocky spur to the west of the town, by the mouth of a little river where shallow-drafted boats can moor.

Once inside the gulf, we head for a little rocky promontory surmounted by a Genoese tower, protecting a bay which provides the best shelter on the whole of the west coast. Having anchored, straightened things out and relaxed for a bit, one can go ashore and wander about. There are a few houses, a little church and a castle surrounded by the shrubby Mediterranean maquis. We can drink in the beauty and heady perfumes, secure in the knowledge that no traffic noise will shatter the peace. Children can have fun making friends with the donkeys that share this peaceful area with the handful of villagers. As evening falls the sunset tinges the rocks with an even deeper red and the sea becomes ever bluer. Then it is time to repair to a restaurant for a delicious dinner.

From Girolata to Propriano   60 nm

The Sanguinaire Islands are situated at the northern edge of the gulf of Ajaccio.

Southward-bound again, we bypass the gulf of Porto with its sheer cliffs. It is dominated to the south by

the massif of the Calanche de Piana, with its spectacular rock formations. After Cape Rosso, the coast changes appearance quite sharply. There are no more high cliffs of red porphyry, but arid grey hills and a much more densely-populated, irregular coastline. Rocky and sandy stretches alternate, providing many possible anchorages. We sail past Cargese and the broad gulf of Sagone. These are not very inspiring and offer no good anchorages. We round Cape Feno, and head for the Sanguinaire Islands which lie at the entrance to the next, deep gulf along this stretch of coast: the Gulf of Ajaccio. These islands are where Alphonse Daudet (1840–97), the French novelist and short-story writer, wrote a chapter of his *Lettres de Mon Moulin*. They are now uninhabited, but they were once given by Genoa to the Ponte family, who were originally from the region of Liguria, "on condition that you plant 800 vines and 600 fruit trees." There are two different interpretations of their sinister name (literally: the Bloody Islands). One is the

AJACCIO AND NAPOLEON

Napoleon Bonaparte's relationship with his native Corsica was far from idyllic. When he returned to the island in 1792 as Lieutenant-Colonel of the French Army, he did not hesitate in firing on his fellow-citizens to suppress Pasquale Paoli's bid for Corsican independence. In spite of this, the white city of Ajaccio is today imbued with a Napoleonic flavour, though it has more to do with tourism than true sentiment. Towards the end of his life, when he was in exile on St Helena, Napoleon remembered his birthplace with regret, saddened by the fact that he had given it "no more than a fountain and a promenade."

Every corner of Ajaccio reminds you of Napoleon: street names, squares, monuments (below) and museums. For those arriving from the sea, the Citadelle port is an ideal starting-point for an itinerary on the subject. From the Cathedral of the "Madonnuccia" (little Madonna), where the infant Napoleon was baptized, and which has a high altar of Italian origin donated by his sister, one goes to Piazza Letizia where there is a statue of Napoleon as a child and to Maison Napoléon (Napoleon's house), a yellow-ocher building. This is now a national museum where one can see furniture and curios including a family tree made with hair. From Rue Bonaparte, a narrow street originally inhabited by Genoese merchants, one emerges into the big rectangular Place Maréchal Foch by the sea-front, with the fountain mentioned above: a monumental structure dedicated to Bonaparte First Consul, with four lions at his feet. The Hôtel de Ville (Town Hall) which faces on to it has a museum dedicated to Napoleon on the first floor, full of documents and portraits of the whole family. Walking back along Cours Napoléon, the main street, after stopping for a coffee at the Café Napoléon, one comes across another colossal monument in Place General de Gaulle: an equestrian figure of Napoleon surrounded by four brothers. To complete the picture, one should go to Place d'Austerlitz where our hero is portrayed in his most familiar pose: one hand tucked into the lapel of his frock-coat and a two-cornered hat on head. (This is a copy of the original which is housed at Les Invalides in Paris.) If you have any energy left, you can visit the Fesch museum where cardinal Fesch, an uncle of Napoleon, collected some beautiful works of art, mainly Italian.

belief, unsubstantiated by evidence, that there were once leper colonies there and the other is that it is a derivation of "Sagonaria," because they are situated near the gulf of Sagone. It seems much more likely that the islands' name comes from the blood red colour which the rocks assume at sunset. This is the best time to view them, passing through the strait if the weather is fine. Otherwise it is better to sail to the south of Tabernacolo rock and head for Ajaccio which has a safe harbour.

Ajaccio is a lively town and is of particular interest to those interested in Napoleon. The best course of action on arrival at Ajaccio is to moor in the Citadelle tourist port, near the old quarter. The Port des Cannes further north is pretty and is about 1 km (⅔ mile) from the center of town.

After Ajaccio, it is best to head straight for the high cliffs of Cape Muro. The square lighthouse – white with a black top – stands on the cliffs. Then we sail into the broad, deep gulf of Valinco. Before reaching Propriano at the end of the gulf, which is our destination for this leg of the journey, we have to pass Porto Pollo point. It is low, rocky and bordered by treacherous rocks. One can stop at Porto Pollo

Above: Propriano is the least picturesque harbour on the west coast, but the northern side of the gulf of Propriano has some lovely anchorages. Porto Pollo in particular, with its dazzling sandy beaches, is an ideal spot at which to moor.

Overleaf: when the west wind gets up, the coast is buffeted by waves. Many bays are open to the prevailing wind and the only safe refuges are the harbours.

FILITOSA

The prehistoric site of Filitosa is situated 5 km (3 miles) inland from Porto Pollo on the north coast of the gulf of Valinco, along a road which follows the course of the river Taravo. It is the result of an extraordinary piece of collaboration between the owner of the land and the archaeologist Grosjean. It consists of menhirs (see illustration below), or monuments from the megalithic culture which followed the Neolithic Age, and was established in Corsica between 3500 and 1000 B.C. These have been positioned in a very interesting pattern. One can also see the remains of a Torrean settlement established between 1500 and 800 B.C. The Torreani were also thought to be responsible for building the nuraghi in Sardinia. This is an enchanting spot and it is worth spending some time here in a setting of olive trees, rushing streams and grazing cows,

admiring Filitosa, the largest menhir, a figure which seems to be carrying a sword and a dagger; the fortified Oppidum, where the Torreani re-used some of the megaliths such as Filitosa IX and Filitosa XIV, and the five standing stones positioned around a thousand-year-old olive tree on the other side of the little valley. After contemplating the mysteries of the remote past and questioning these ancient stones on the enigma of human existence, one can visit the museum where various items which were dug up are displayed. These include the Scalza Murta menhir, a representation of a human figure which predates archaic Greek statuary; Filitosa XII, a menhir representing a human figure with the left arm and hand outlined, and a famous head known as Tappa II. The latter has an extraordinary archetypal face, with a priestly air, barely outlined features, and a mouth set in an arcane smile which seems to have a message for us from the past.

bay, at the mouth of the river Taravo. This is a good place to shelter from the mistral and an ideal starting-point for an excursion to the archaeological site of Filitosa.

Overleaf: Bonifacio harbour is situated at the end of a fjord, sheltered from all winds. The main wharf is crowded with bars and restaurants.

From Propriano to Bonifacio 40 nm

Propriano is a busy tourist resort which has developed over the last few decades. It has a sheltered harbour with good shops and ample opportunity to replenish stores. After Propriano, Campomoro bay provides a lovely anchorage which is sheltered from the libeccio (south-west wind) but not the mistral. After rounding Punta di Campomoro, the coast becomes rocky and arid, and surmounted by bare hills. It is best to keep well out to sea, as there are dangerous rocks offshore. If the sun is shining and you wish to stop, there is a magnificent beach at Conca bay with crystal-clear water. But beware: after Cape Senetosa the coast curves sharply south-eastwards and one comes under the influence of the Straits of Bonifacio. It is necessary to consult the shipping and weather forecasts very carefully, as the channelled winds will be much more powerful and can cause strong currents. The coast is craggy here, and composed of pink and white granite which is reminiscent of Sardinia. Mediterranean maquis is practically the only type of vegetation. There are plenty of anchorages to choose from in good weather, although they are not usually sheltered from west winds. Shoals and other hazards along this coast call for careful navigation. After passing La Botte rock, we come to two fine bays, the gulfs of Mortoli and Roccapina. The latter has a beautiful beach of white sand, with a very pretty sheltered cove on the north side which has room for only a few boats with a draft of not more than 2 m (6 ft 6 in). After three or four more attractive bays, Figari, with the Cagna mountains visible in the distance, offers the only safe shelter along this stretch of coast. This inlet is more than 2 miles long, and the waves gradually lose their force before reaching the end of the bay, where the few buildings are well-camouflaged by the dense undergrowth. There is the usual Genoese tower, known as Figari tower, and three or four inlets along the shore where one can anchor after carefully inspecting the seabed for the numerous rocks and shallows. After Figari bay we head for Cape Feno, a

Below: the west coast has beaches of very fine, white sand and is ideal for swimming and sunbathing.

promontory surmounted by a heavy block of granite beyond Punta di Ventilegne. Paragnano bay is a good place to stop in fine weather and is interesting geologically, because it marks a clear boundary between the area of pink granite and that of white limestone. Its west side is pink, while the east is white. Immediately afterwards is the little creek of Fazzio, which has a yachting center. We have now reached Bonifacio. As though someone had uttered the words "Open Sesame," the entrance to a fjord carved out of white limestone appears before us. Beyond the imposing entrance, the furies of the strait abate as if by magic, giving way to a wonderful calm. Bonifacio has always been part of the sea, isolated from the arid, inhospitable terrain that surrounds it. It was founded in 828 by Marquis Bonifacio of Lucca on his return from a journey to the Holy Land. Since then, it has had a history of piracy, relentless sieges, acts of loyalty, heroism and betrayal. It was bitterly contested on account of its strategic position, finally passing from Genoa to France with the rest of Corsica. Remaining true to its tough reputation, Bonifacio had a detachment of the Foreign Legion garrisoned in the citadel until 1983. It can be hard to find room in the tourist port at the end of the fjord in the high season. However, as it is a very good, well-equipped port, it is worth arriving early in the morning. Before leaving the harbour, one should take a walk around the impregnable looking citadel on the limestone promontory between the fjord and the sea, which is deeply eroded at the base. A visit to the aquarium built imaginatively inside a cave on the Quai Comparetti is a must. There, one can admire the rare and brilliantly coloured species which live in the sea around Corsica. You can go from the darkness of a cave to the bright light of the panorama at the top of the citadel, where a view stretches for miles over the fabulous scenery of the Straits, and embraces a sizeable portion of the Gallura region on the Sardinian coast. From this vantage point, one can see a number of interesting architectural features, such as the silos which could store enough grain to feed the population for months in times of siege and a series of arches connecting the buildings, which carried rainwater from a communal cistern into a system of tanks. The sumptuous palaces contrast with the individual tall, narrow houses in the old quarter. At one time, access to these was by step ladders which could be removed

LAVEZZI

Not to visit Lavezzi and the surrounding area would be unpardonable given the wild beauty of this little archipelago and the fact that it is only about five miles from Bonifacio. Lavezzi is part of a nature reserve which includes rocks and the little islands surrounding it (see below), such as Isola Piana, Ratin, Poraggia and Perduto rock. It is a magical world of pink granite smoothed into sinuous curves by thousands of years of vigorous polishing by the wind and waves of the Straits. Patches of vegetation have rooted themselves in the crevices and rare plant species like the sand lily and arum fly-trap can be seen. The fauna includes unusual reptiles and amphibians and sea-birds such as cormorants, common gulls, shearwaters and Corsican gulls, which are smaller than the normal type. The island is very rocky and indented, with various possible anchorages which should be cautiously approached with the aid of detailed charts. Two small cemeteries and the Sémillante Pyramid are a stern reminder of the dangers of the place. They recall a tragedy which occurred on this stretch of coast a century ago. In 1885, the French frigate *Sémillante*, bound for the Crimea with 750 soldiers on board, was wrecked off the island in a violent storm and there were no survivors. Only a priest witnessed the tragedy. Alphonse Daudet, the French writer, dedicated a chapter of his *Lettres de Mon Moulin* to the subject. A century later, the simple little cemeteries seem to add to the attraction of the island, as if the people who perished there were at

least fortunate in finding such a beautiful place for their eternal rest. Of the possible anchorages, Lazarina is quite large and well sheltered, but usually very crowded. It is bounded to the southwest by the rocks on which the Sémillante pyramid stands and it is a good place to spend the night.

Farther on is Giunco anchorage, open to the south-east, and less well sheltered from westerlies. Here there is one of the two cemeteries; the other is at the end of Greco anchorage opposite, on the eastern side and facing the east wind. The latter is preferable when the west wind blows. If it is overcrowded, one can stop at the bay a little further to the west. Chiasa, a solitary creek between granite masses, lies to the north-west. It is very attractive and well sheltered from all winds, and there is a little beach at the end.

These islands were once heavily populated, particularly Lavezzi. The inhabitants were shepherds, farmers and, in Roman times, a colony of slaves who quarried granite there. The inhabitants were eventually driven away by pirates.

Nearby is Cavallo, which has a very different atmosphere. The fauna which has settled there recently, thanks to the money which has been spent on establishing and protecting it, is also different. This island is the haunt of the jet set, and boasts luxury villas, a little hotel and a landing strip.

to protect the occupants from intruders. The inhabitants must have lived in constant fear of siege, for to enter the citadel through its only gate, Porta Genova, one had to pass through no fewer than eight others which were guarded by sentries. They were locked by the Podestà (chief magistrate) every evening.

From Bonifacio to Porto Vecchio   25 nm

If the mistral is blowing when we leave Bonifacio, it will carry us swiftly out of the Straits. One must be very careful and follow the navigational instructions exactly, to avoid running into one of the numerous rocks or shoals which endanger the route until beyond Isola Piana. Having rounded Cape Pertusato, the southernmost point of Corsica, 80 m (262 ft) high, where there is one of the most powerful lighthouses in the Mediterranean, watch out for the Prete shoal which lies 400 m (437 yds) from the coast.

After Punta Sprono, heading north-east, we sail through the Piantarella strait, leaving Isola Piana to port and Tignosa di Ratino and the perils of Poraggia island to starboard. To avoid trouble it is best to follow the nautical instructions and keep between the beacons of Isola Piana and Punta Sprono. (In poor visibility, it is better to use the wide channel of the Straits of Bonifacio between the islands of Lavezzi and Razzoli, making a detour round Lavezzi and Cavallo islands.) There is a good anchorage north of Punta Sprono between the coast and the southern tip of Isola Piana. One cannot continue northwards between Isola Piana and the coast: there is no way through.

After Punta Capicciolo, we come to the Gulf of Santa Manza, where mussels are farmed. It slopes from south-west to north-east and is sheltered from all except the east and north-east winds. The gulf is quite peaceful and thinly populated, except by a few summer campers on the south coast. The round bay of Rondinara about 3 miles north of Punta Capicciolo is much more attractive. Continuing north for about three miles, we come to the unspoiled little bay of Porto Nuovo, which is sheltered from westerlies. The pink of the granite cliffs is reflected over the surface of the water and the two deserted beaches which are separated by a small headland. These beaches are empty because they are inaccessible from

the mainland. Continuing northwards, 6 miles before Punta di a Chiappa, we come to the beautiful Gulf of Santa Giulia, which has been ruined by tourism. One can avoid it by sailing between the rocky coast and the Cerbicale islands. This little archipelago, which includes Isola Piana and Maestro Maria, is part of a nature reserve inhabited by seabirds, reptiles and small mammals. It has a few anchorages which are good in fine weather, but one cannot land on the islands between 1 April and 31 August. Finally, we round Punta di a Chiappa, a 60-m (197-ft) high bluff and, passing between Chiapino rock and dry land, enter the gulf of Porto Vecchio, sailing along a well-marked channel for another 4 miles.

The south coast of the gulf has two other good

On pages 166 and 167: the vivid colours of the sea, sky and flowers contrast with the pale grey of Genoese-style houses of the town of Bonifacio which in turn blend into the sheer cliffs on which they are built.

anchorages. These are Marina D'Archi and Ziglione islet. Hidden by Punta di U Cerchiu, Porto Vecchio awaits us at the end. It is an attractive port with a fascinating history. The remains of the citadel and the old city gate are at the top of a little hill of porphyry which climbs straight up from the harbour. It was a thriving settlement in antiquity, because of its huge cork oak forests and salt-works. But many of the valleys of Corsica were neglected over time and this caused the river to become silted up, producing a swamp and, subsequently malaria. In the sixteenth century Genoa built a citadel there, although time and again her enforced settlements succumbed to malaria. Since the war Porto Vecchio has been transformed into a busy resort.

The coast near Porto Vecchio is craggy, becoming low and sandy farther on. There stand former Genoese watch-towers, built to forewarn the inhabitants of enemies approaching from the sea.

THE GULF OF LIONS AND THE BALEARICS

St Tropez–Porquerolles–Cassis–
Port-Camargue–Sète–Cadaqués–Puerto
de Mahon–Palma de Mallorca–Ibiza

This is a classic cruise, one of the most beautiful in the western Mediterranean. It combines varied and beautiful scenery with stimulating visits to French and Spanish towns which are full of history and fascinating traditions, and at the same time, modern and dynamic.

The area between the southernmost point of the Côte d'Azur and Formentera, the furthermost island in the Balearics, is the realm of the mistral (north-west wind). This is one of the strongest winds in the Mediterranean and, although it blows with less force in summer, crossing the famous Gulf of Lions adds a touch of danger to the voyage which makes it all the more exciting.

From St Tropez to Ibiza

The battlements of the ancient castle of Tossa de Mar on the Costa Brava, set against sunlit cliffs, topped by dark green trees and shrubs – a classic image of what is perhaps the most beautiful coast on the Mediterranean. This itinerary combines breathtaking scenery with visits to towns of great cultural and historical interest.

St Tropez boasts all the qualities of this cruise itinerary. It is a lively and sophisticated resort, set in a beautiful, natural deep bay. Everyone knows that it is frequented by the rich and famous. But how many are familiar with the Annonciade museum, situated near the harbour, which houses an interesting collection of works by modern artists, from Matisse to Utrillo?

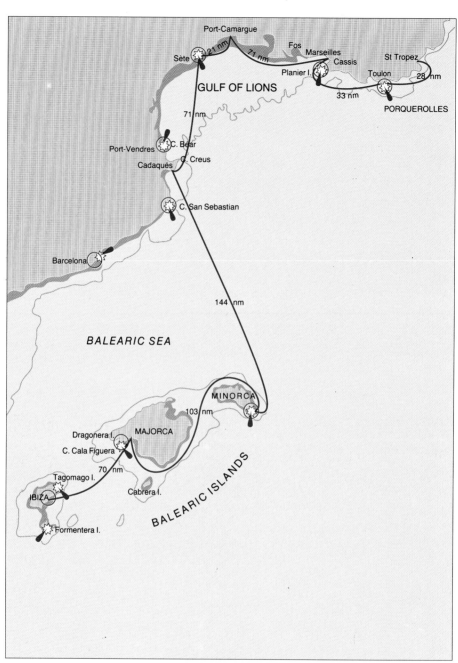

Port-Camargue
Fos
Sète 21 nm
Marseilles
71 nm
St Tropez
Cassis
GULF OF LIONS
Planier I.
Toulon
28 nm
33 nm
PORQUEROLLES

71 nm
Port-Vendres C. Bear
C. Creus
Cadaqués

C. San Sebastian

Barcelona

144 nm

BALEARIC SEA

MINORCA
103 nm
Dragonera I. MAJORCA
C. Cala Figuera
70 nm
Tagomago I.
Cabrera I.
IBIZA
BALEARIC ISLANDS
Formentera I.

Distance covered: 541 nm.
Average temperatures: St Tropez: 24°C (75.2°F) in July and August; Balearics: 25°C (77°F) in July and August.
Prevailing winds: the mistral (NW), often strong.
Cartography: British Admiralty:

1705 (Cabo to San Sebastian to Iles d'Hyeres); 2606 (Approaches to Sète); 1506 (Plans on the S. coast of France); 1704 (Punta de la Bana to Islas Medos); 1703 (Majorca and Minorca); 1702 (Ibiza, Formentera and Southern Majorca). Istituto Idrografico

Italiano: 340 (general).
Bibliography: South France Pilot (Imray Laurie Norie & Wilson); East Spain Pilot, Islas Baleares (Imray Laurie Norie & Wilson); Baedeker's Ibiza, Majorca and Minorca (Automobile Association).

Leaving the bay, we sail past Cape Camarat and head out to sea towards Porquerolles, in the Iles d'Hyères (Hyères islands). The island of Porquerolles, with its modern marina and nineteenth century village, and the island of Port-Cros, now a nature reserve, have fragrant eucalyptus woods, silent little bays and dazzling beaches. They seem to belong to another age, with their unspoiled beauty and total absence of motor cars.

Cassis is an attractive little town just east of Marseilles. It is famous for its white cliffs, its crustaceans, the poetry of Frédéric Mistral and the paintings of Matisse and Dufy. It is at the center of the "calanques": dramatic clefts in the rocks along the coast, which one can explore by boat, or with boots and crampons if one is an expert climber.

Having consulted the forecasts in the harbour office, we venture into the heart of the Gulf of Lions, by the Rhône delta, where the mistral rises. The Camargue is an expanse of sandy beaches, swamps inhabited by pink flamingoes, cane-thickets and meadows where the famous white horses graze. The marina at Port-Camargue is the ideal place to leave the boat before making an excursion to the fortified

The Balearics are the destination of our final cruise itinerary, which crosses the famous Gulf of Lions. Despite the growth of tourism, these islands off the Spanish coasts have not lost their appeal. Even on the most built-up island, Majorca, there are still some beautiful unspoiled bays like Cala Guya (below).

town of Aigues-Mortes, to Saintes-Maries-de-la-Mer, where a traditional gypsy festival is held at the end of May, and to Arles, which has the finest Roman arena in Provence. One can alternate visits to the towns with horse riding and the sampling of delicious Provençal cuisine.

On the east coast of the gulf is Sète. It is a little town situated between the sea and the silver waters of Etang du Roi, famous for its water tournaments and oyster farms.

Then we head for the imposing rocks of Cape Creus, which marks the boundary between France and Spain. A stop at Cadaqués, with its little white houses and interesting cathedral, provides a brief introduction to Catalonia, before the long stretch to the Balearics. The town's architecture has been influenced by nearby Figueras, home of Salvador Dalí.

The Balearic islands are wonderfully situated, and enjoy a particularly good climate. It is easy to understand why the earliest Mediterranean settlers were attracted to them.

Here too, the beautiful scenery is made all the more interesting by traces of ancient cultures. At Minorca, one can admire the fjord-like inlet of Puerto de Mahon, the spectacular Bronze Age ruins, the lush green landscape of the interior, and the unspoiled town of Ciudadela.

Palma de Mallorca also boasts fine architectural features and historical remains, hidden among the colossal new buildings. These are a striking contrast to the steps and slopes of Pollensa, a picturesque village at the north of the island, and the charm of Cabrera, a little island south of Majorca, which is dominated by the ruins of an old castle.

Ibiza is covered in trees and has numerous springs. It attracts visitors both for its undeniable beauty, and its reputation as an international, cosmopolitan resort. Its harbour is an ideal base from which to tack along the coast, where a stiff breeze ruffles the turquoise sea.

From St Tropez to Porquerolles   28 nm

One should visit St Tropez at least once. It is situated at the south of one of the most beautiful gulfs on the Côte d'Azur. The life of this colourful town is centered around the old harbour with its many *crêperies* selling pancakes and cider.

MARSEILLES

The approach to Marseilles is one of the most picturesque sights in the western Mediterranean, particularly when this wonderful old town is bathed in the warm colours of sunset. The route takes one past the islands, islets and rocks of the Frioul archipelago which calls for careful navigation.

Marseilles has various tourist ports, but to savour the authentic atmosphere and 25 centuries of history, one should sail right into the Vieux Port at the heart of the old town and step ashore on the cobblestones laid at the time of Louis XII and XIII. Then, first thing in the morning, buy some croissants at one of the bars filled with the aroma of pastis, climb up to Place Notre-Dame-de-la-Garde in the clear light of the mistral, and stroll along La Canebière just as it is coming to life. La Canebière is the most elegant road in the town, studded with luxurious shops. It has become world famous through the tales of the many sailors who travel through each day.

Overleaf: the tough Mediterranean maquis can withstand the powerful blasts of the mistral, which gathers speed as it leaves the valley of the Rhône, often reaching force 9 along this stretch of coast.

Left: Cassis is the elegant little "capital" of the calanques: an area of white cliffs cleft by ravines which form beautiful, wild fjords.

A short distance from the bustling harbour the atmosphere is much more peaceful. One can explore the narrow streets of the old town center, with the splendid Provençal houses, walk to the Baroque church, where there is a gilded wooden bust of St Tropez, and then climb up to the sixteenth-century citadel. It is worth making the effort in order to enjoy the magnificent view of the town, gulf and Massif des Maures. Another interesting place to spend an afternoon is the Musée de l'Annonciade, which houses a collection of modern paintings donated by Georges Grammont. Many of these paintings are by famous artists inspired during their sojourn at St Tropez.

There are some good trips to be made in the area. One of the most interesting excursions is to the village of Grimaud, which has a ruined castle. Just outside the bay, the low promontory of Cape St Tropez extends to starboard. On the north side is a sandy shoreline overlooked by a few villas. The most popular beach is in the bay of Pampelonne.

Beyond the picturesque Cape Camarat, the coast becomes craggy and indented, with a few sheltered beaches where the mistral does not penetrate. Then it bends sharply northwards, opening into the deep Bay of Cavalaire. Our itinerary, however, takes us south-west, towards Porquerolles. We therefore leave the islands of the Levant, Port-Cros and Bagaud to the south, and sail on across the turquoise sea. This stretch of water is sheltered from the waves of the mistral, but we can still benefit from the wind in our sails. Porquerolles is separated from the other islands in the archipelago by a channel about 5½ miles long, called the Grande Passe. The harbour lies in a natural cove at the center of the north coast of the island.

From Porquerolles to Cassis 33 nm

Porquerolles is perhaps the loveliest port of call on the south coast of France. We are welcomed to the island by the strongly-scented bouquet of umbrella pines, eucalyptus, bougainvillea, myrtle, fennel and lavender.

At the foot of the hill of Sante-Agathe little white houses line the large rectangular Place d'Armes, shaded by eucalyptus trees which frame the church of St Anne. Only bicycles pass along the flagged streets.

The best way to see the interior of the island, with

its rich and varied vegetation, is on foot. There are many possible itineraries, one of the best starts from the village and climbs up the hills through the woods. There is a magnificent view of the islands at the top.

About 1 km (⅔ mile) west of the village, is Bon Renaud with Plage d'Argent, a long, "silver" beach with exceptionally clear water. A little farther on is Aiguadon, a wild, rocky inlet with three beaches and sparkling water. One of the most famous anchorages is in Langoustier bay, at the far west of the island.

The south-east side of Porquerolles has some of the most picturesque spots in the archipelago, in which rugged cliffs, often virtually inaccessible by land, suddenly give way to little beaches where peace and quiet are guaranteed. One such spot is the long, narrow inlet of Breganconnet, which ends in a tiny beach furrowed by a trickle of spring water.

Then the coast rises, like a natural fortress. Just before Cap d'Armes is a tiny cove called the Gorge du Loup, which is very good for subaqua fishing, as is l'Indienne, another little bay symmetrical to the Gorge du Loup, to the east of the squat promontory on which the Porquerolles lighthouse stands.

The north coast stretches before us after we have rounded Cape Mèdes and its rocks. This coast has the best beaches, including Notre-Dame, which has golden sand and is the most popular because it is sheltered from the mistral and easily accessible from the village.

From Porquerolles to Cassis we follow the coast. The force of the mistral is broken by the many bays, but the gentle breeze makes the air wonderfully clear. We cross the Petite Passe and emerge opposite the Giens peninsula at one side of the gulf of Toulon (the rocky Cape Scié is at the other). We leave the light-coloured buildings of Bandol, l'Île Rousse and l'Île Verte to starboard, then a distinctive red spur, the Bec d'Aigle, marks the beginning of a short stretch of tall, regular cliffs ending in the bay of Cassis.

Cassis is visible from afar. A picturesque old town with a cheerful, lively fishing port, it is dominated by a medieval castle and somewhat dwarfed to the north-west by large villas and hotels. The main attraction of this town is as a base from which to visit the famous *calanques* by boat or on foot.

Between Cassis and Marseilles, the coast is dominated by the limestone massif of Marseilleveyre. This

On pages 180 and 181: as the sun sinks below the horizon, it sets the waters of l'Etang de la Ville on fire. The Camargue has a fascinating, distinctive charm.

Between the two branches of the Rhône along the coastal portion of the Camargue are the salt-works of Giroud. Dazzling mountains of salt stand out against an otherwise flat landscape.

is covered in maquis, which thins out and disappears as the rocks drop sheer to the sea, revealing bare limestone cliffs and ravines, which change colour with the light. They are yellow in the morning, dazzling white in the midday sun and a dramatic pink and violet at sunset. This is the best time to linger in the calanques, when the boats which ply back and forth during the day have gone, the water regains its clarity and the shadows emphasize the clefts in the rocks. The nearest calanque to Cassis is Port-Miou. This long, narrow "gorge" with a zigzag entrance which shuts out all winds, extends for 1 km (⅔ mile) between the sheer cliffs.

The most beautiful calanque is En-Vau. It shares an entrance with Port Pin but branches off to the north-west. It is 150 m (500 ft) wide to begin with, but expands and contracts with almost geometrical regularity for 600 m (656 yds) between two vertiginous walls of white rock, finally ending in a little beach.

Morgiou and Sormiou enclose two little harbours.

The first calanque is very wide at the entrance, then narrows sharply towards the end, where the harbour lies, surrounded by a little fishing village. The second calanque is quite wide for a long stretch, then splits up into two little bays. The one to the north has a tiny harbour, while the one to the west has a village clustered about it.

From Cassis to Port-Camargue   71 nm

The Camargue has seventy miles of shoreline. This area is battered by the wind. The mistral sweeps across every bay and it means some hard sailing with the vessel close-hauled. After the big bay of Marseilles, dominated by the Planier lighthouse, one of the largest in the Mediterranean, the high cliffs slope westwards as far as Cape Couronne. This is a bare and flat promontory opening into the deep gulf of Fos, where there are large industrial plants. From this point, the land to the west becomes invisible

PORT-CROS

This looks like a pirates' island. In fact, up until two centuries ago, Port-Cros was the lair of dreaded corsairs, who attacked sailing ships bound for the Côte d'Azur and Liguria, in Italy. It is an ideal place for a day's cruise, but watch the weather reports: the mistral makes it difficult and often dangerous to moor in the little harbour.

The island is covered in luxurious vegetation. Like the island of Bagaud – where one is forbidden to land – it is a nature reserve. The main attractions of Port-Cros are the scenic walks inland. However, the deep bay of Port-Man, to the east facing the Île du Levant, and the grotto at Cognet Point at the far south-west of the island, are two places worth exploring by boat.

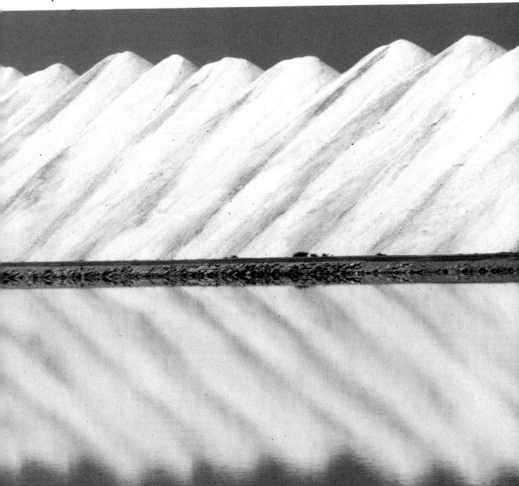

THE FERRADES

In the Camargue, one can attend the "ferrades" (the ceremonial branding of young bulls), and other traditional festivals.

The most famous takes place at the end of May, at Saintes-Maries-de-la-Mer. This charming little village is built around a fortified church. One can now go there by boat, as a new harbour, Port Gardian, was built in 1984 (before that, one could only stop there in fine weather). According to legend, the three Marys and their servant Sarah (patron saint of gypsies) landed here in A.D. 40. Their tomb is now a place of pilgrimage for gypsies the world over, and colourful festivals are held there twice yearly. Statues of the saints are carried through the streets (see below), along the beach and into the sea. Equestrian shows and bull fights are held and the "gardians" (herdsmen) and "arlésiens" (citizens of Arles) wear traditional costumes.

A few kilometers inland from Saintes-Maries, the proud bastions of the fortified town of Aigues-Mortes rise up from the melancholy landscape of salt lakes and marshes. This is a perfectly-preserved medieval town, which is still surrounded by its original walls.

from the open sea, and is bordered with very long sandy beaches.

Port-Camargue is a modern tourist port somewhat lacking in character. But it is the only sensible place to leave the boat if one is to explore this desert of sand and salt lakes. There one can see grey herons, pink flamingoes and rare species of migrant bird which nest in the wildest area between the two branches of the Rhône. This has been a nature reserve for more than 20 years. Here, one can still find "manades," or herds of bulls managed by "gardians," who ride the beautiful white horses of the Camargue.

From Port-Camargue to Sète   21 nm

Leaving Le Grau-du-Roi, the coast continues westwards, low, straight, and punctuated by the ugly, modern white pyramids of La Grande Motte. The first mountain to break the low horizon of sandy beaches is Mont St-Clair, at the base of which lies Sète.

"Je suis né dans un de ces lieux ou j'aurais aimé naître" (I was born in just the type of place where I should like to have been born) said the poet Paul Valéry of his native town, Sète. The oldest and most picturesque part of Sète lies between the Canal de Sète and the harbour, which was built in the seventeenth century on the orders of Colbert, Chief Minister to Louis XIV. It is full of fishing boats, tourists and very good fish and seafood restaurants. One should visit the marine cemetery overlooking the sea, where Valéry was buried. Fort St-Pierre below it has a drama festival every year. The Corniche promenade along the seafront leads to Mont St-Clair. From the Chapel of Notre-Dame-de-la-Salette, one can see the Pyrenees beyond the sea and lakes. Another breathtaking sight is the Etang de Thau, a silver lagoon cut off from the sea by a spit of land. On the north coast are fishermen's villages where oysters are farmed. These oysters are famous, and are know as the "huîtres de Bouzigues." Not to be missed are the "joutes nautiques" (centuries-old nautical jousting tournaments).

From Sète to Cadaqués   71 nm

Then we set sail again, bound for the Costa Brava, perhaps with the mistral in our favour. The coast

PROVENÇAL CUISINE

Few culinary traditions comply with modern recommendations about diet as closely as the cuisine of Provence, with its preference for olive oil, fish and lighter foods in general, and abundant use of garlic. Conversely, towards Montpellier and the Languedoc region, the cooking is rather heavy, with dishes such as "cassoulet toulousain" (a stew made from pork, sausage, lamb, goose fat and beans).

Famous Provençal specialities include stuffed vegetables, "salade niçoise," "ratatouille" and "bouillabaisse" (the world-famous aromatic fish stew), which is always served with a garlic-flavoured mayonnaise called "rouille." In Nice, one should try "pistou" (a vegetable minestrone of Genoese origins).

Lobsters and other crustaceans, and every imaginable type of fish are eaten. Distinctive flavours include "anchoïade" (anchovy paste) and "brandade" (creamed salt cod, originating from Nîmes).

The types of meat eaten (see below) are from small and medium-sized animals: rabbit ("terrine de lapereau" is a typical dish); lamb; pork; poultry and game, often accompanied by fruit. Desserts include figs flavoured with vanilla, "clafoutis" (fruit baked in batter), Montélimar (nougat) and candied fruit.

Excellent wines are produced in Provence, including famous names like Châteauneuf du Pape and the white Cassis. Côtes de Provence rosé is also good, and is produced by wine-growing cooperatives throughout the area.

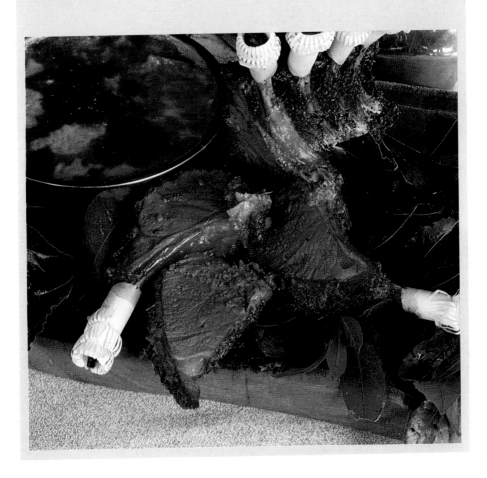

CATALAN CUISINE

Garlic and olive oil also figure largely in Catalan cuisine. The area is famous for the latter, Borjas Blancas in Catalonia being one of two Spanish regions where olive oil is regulated like wine. Typical recipes with garlic are "sopa di ajo" (garlic soup) and "allioli" (a sauce served with meat and vegetables).

The Catalan people are fond of stews made with meat, like "escudella in carn d'olla" (with a mixture of boiled meats), or fish, crustaceans and seafood. All menus include seafood dishes like "zarzuela de mariscos," "sopa de peix" with soft breadcrumbs or "suquet," or, richest of all, "peix a la badalonina" with octopus, cuttlefish, squid and vegetables. Lobster is typically served "a la romescu" (with wine and almond sauce). Rice ("arrøz") is very popular. The local "arroz a la catalana" is a close relative of the ubiquitous "paella" from Valencia.

Meat dishes tend to be quite hearty: "cordero" (lamb) and "cochinillo asado" (roast suckling pig) are especially recommended, plus even more substantial dishes like "butifarra amb monjetes" (black sausage with white beans or "judias" – green beans) and "lomillo" (pork fillet with beans or "setas" – mushrooms). Poultry and game dishes are also very good and fairly elaborate e.g. "oca amb peres" (goose with pears), stuffed duck, and partridge with Brussels sprouts.

The Catalans love sweets: "crema catalana" (a kind of cream caramel which is served tepid) and "blanc menjar" (almond milk sprinkled with cinnamon) are typical examples.

The wines of this hot, fertile region are usually quite potent. The white Alella is best with fish, being not too dry, and "Priorato" or "Perelada" go well with meat. The muscatel, produced throughout Catalonia, is also delicious, and the local spirit, made in Tarragona, will make a fitting end to your meal.

continues low and sandy for about 40 miles, with seaside resorts visible at intervals. Then it dramatically changes appearance at the Spanish border. The eastern slopes of the Pyrenees, some of whose peaks are over 1,000 m (3,280 ft) high, drop to the sea, forming the dark, rocky promontories of Cape Béar and Cape Creus, with the white village of Cadaqués visible between them.

We are now on the Costa Brava, one of the most beautiful parts of the Western Mediterranean. It has an exceptionally wide choice of safe anchorages, and there are numerous deserted inlets where unspoiled villages set like jewels in green bays still retain their old world charm.

Cape Creus, the easternmost point of Spain, opens into a series of picturesque bays: Cala Portalo, with dark, tortuous rocks, devoid of vegetation; Cala de

Overleaf: Cadaqués consists of a cluster of white houses at the end of a bay, in a beautiful natural setting.

The sheer, pink and white limestone cliffs of the calanques attract many tourists and rock-climbers. The best time to view them is therefore at dawn or dusk, when their wild beauty is undisturbed.

Culip, with its lunar landscape of uneven black rocks and little yachting harbour; Cala Fragosa; Cala Fredosa; Cala Jugadora; Cala Bona and Cala Guillola, where gentle hills alternate with austere valleys, and craggy rock-falls contrast with smooth, inviting beaches.

Cadaqués consists of a cluster of houses nestling at the end of a broad bay with two beaches where the fishermen leave their boats in the evening. It is an exceptionally beautiful setting, and the many buildings which have been added to the nucleus of the old village have not spoiled its indolent charm.

On the north side of the promontory is Port Lligat, the fishing village where there is the family house of the artist Salvador Dalì. For those not content with a visit to the villa, which has many ingenious architectural features and was extended over the years by Dalì, Figueras is not far away. Torre Galatea, Dalì's shrine to his wife Gala, and the nearby museum dedicated to him, where Dali is buried, contain about 700 works by this extraordinary man.

From Cadaqués to Puerto de Mahon   144 nm

The stretch from Cadaqués to Minorca is not so long as to be daunting, but it is long enough for one to appreciate the thrill of sailing for some hours out of sight of land.

In clear weather, Minorca can be seen from a distance of several miles, a rocky, blue plateau with a few higher points. Entering the long, fjord-like inlet which leads to Mahon, the main port on the island, and feeling the sea steadily grow calmer between its green banks is an unforgettable experience, particularly after a very rough crossing.

Minorca is the most picturesque island in the Balearics – the softest and greenest. It was governed by the British in the eighteenth century and Admiral Lord Nelson was said to have stayed at Golden Farm, which is visible against the green hill as one enters the fjord. The island is small enough to circumnavigate in a few days, but one will probably be tempted to linger in the deserted narrow inlets. The three harbours at Mahon, Ciudadela and Fornells are all pleasant and provide good shelter in all weathers.

Salvador Dalì spent a great deal of time at Cadaqués, his home town, leaving his mark on the local architecture. This is the façade of a "modernist" house.

ARLES

The town of Arles at the northern edge of the Camargue plain is steeped in history and has outstanding examples of Provençal art. It is at the center of the region where the traditional "langue d'oc" is still spoken, and has two of the most important Roman monuments in France: an arena and a theater. Other interesting Roman remains include the portal and cloisters of the Church of St Trophime. A little way from the center are Les Alyscamps: an ancient Roman necropolis and subsequently a medieval Christian cemetery, which has proved a source of inspiration for poets and painters.

These included Van Gogh, who lived and worked at Arles in 1880. The blazing sun and colourful scenery of Provence persuaded him to abandon impressionist ideas and develop his own, distinctive style of painting. Van Gogh continued to paint the fishermen, peasants and landscapes of Provence until his death in 1890. One of his most famous pictures is of the drawbridge at Arles (below).

ARCHAEOLOGY IN THE BALEARICS

The history of the Balearics is an ancient one, and the island of Minorca shows many traces of former civilizations. The earliest evidence of an advanced culture dates from the Bronze Age, in the first millennium B.C. This consists of more than 200 "talayots," or towers in the form of truncated pyramids built of huge blocks of stone, and more than four hundred "taulas," vertical stones with a horizontal stone placed on top of them. Little is known about them. Near Ciudadela, on Minorca, is the Naveta d'es Tudons, the oldest megalithic monument in the Balearics. Cala'n Porter, 10 km (6 miles) west of Mahon, has prehistoric cave dwellings in its cliffs. Santanyi, 16 km (10 miles) south of Felanitx on Majorca, still has the remains of prehistoric fortifications. Items from the excavations can be seen at the museum at Palma de Mallorca.

It is certain that the Phoenicians landed and stayed at the islands, as can be seen from the huge necropolis near Ibiza. But the Carthaginians were the first true colonizers of the area. They established a trading center on Ibiza in the seventh century B.C. The temple at Cuyeram cave near Santa Eulalia del Rio dates from that period, as does the huge necropolis at Puig des Molins. A bust of the goddess Talit was found here, which is now housed in the archaeological museum at Ibiza.

The Romans succeeded the Carthaginians in 123 B.C.; evidence of their culture can be seen in the amphitheater south of the town of Alcudia and in the town of Inca, which had a large colonial settlement. These are both on Majorca. San Antonio Abad on Ibiza was another Roman town, known as Portus Magnus. After the fall of the Roman Empire, the Balearics were invaded by the Vandals, Byzantines and Goths, who left no traces until the Christian king Jaime I of Aragon conquered them between 1229 and 1235.

From Puerto de Mahon to Palma de Mallorca   103 nm

The first place to explore is the fjord of Puerto de Mahon, which offers a lot of good moorings. The most attractive is Cala Teulera, a long, narrow bay between the little island of El Lazareto and La Mola peninsula.

Just south of the entrance to the sound, Cala de Sant Esteban reaches a long way inshore, flanked by pretty white fishermen's cottages.

To the north is one of the most famous natural harbours in the archipelago, Cala d'Addaya. The

entrance to this long inlet is protected by a group of rocky islets and partially obstructed by shoals. Parallel to Cala d'Addaya is Cala Moli, which is overlooked by the white village of Na Macaret.

At the center of the northern part of the island is the deep Bay of Fornells, surrounded by rugged hills. The village of Fornells is dominated by a hill perforated with caves. It is a picturesque fishing village of ancient origin, where lobsters are now farmed. They are a speciality of the island and are eaten with the famous "mahonesa" (mayonnaise, invented in Mahon).

After rounding Cape Caballería, along the coast to

Fornells, one of three safe landing-places on the island of Minorca, is a little fishing village which is dominated by a hill perforated with natural caves. The local speciality is lobster, served with mayonnaise.

BARCELONA

One of the most attractive places in the Mediterranean, Barcelona is the second largest city in Spain and the capital of Catalonia. One can moor at the end of the commercial port, right in the town center. The marinas are well-organized and friendly, encouraging one to stay and spend time wandering through the maze of streets of the Barrio Gótico (the top of the old town). There are some very impressive Gothic buildings to admire, and the city bustles with street musicians, groups dancing the "sardana" and unusual markets.

One can stroll along the Ramblas, where there is one of the finest theaters in Europe, before returning to the Puerta de la Paz which overlooks the sea. There one can see a replica of Christopher Columbus' ship Santa Maria, or admire the tireless imagination of Antoni Gaudí in the Sagrada Familia (Church of the Holy Family), or the monumental "Cascade" with groups in bronze and stone by Gaudí and other artists in the Ciudadela Park. Art lovers should not miss the Picasso and Miró museums and the museum of Catalonian art. Lovers of good food can tuck into an enormous paella, washed down with sangría.

the west of Fornells, practically deserted and peppered with rocks, we come to some of the most beautiful inlets on the island: Puerto Nitge, a narrow inlet surrounded by a rocky shore and barren hills with dry-stone walls; Cala Pregonda, a bay with crystal-clear water surrounded by a shady wood, a sandy beach and a few jagged rocks which assume fiery tints at sunset; and the two creeks of Algayarens, between tall cliffs and very popular in the summer.

Having rounded Cape Menorca, the westernmost point of the island, we enter the narrow inlet of Ciudadela, a natural harbour which stretches inland for over a kilometer (⅔ mile). This lively, picturesque town is built on a cliff overlooking the port. Ciudadela is the ancient capital of the island of Minorca, and has the dignity of a sixteenth-century fortified town. Below the Gothic cathedral is the maze of streets of the medieval quarter, interrupted here and there by picturesque vaulting and aristocratic façades. Traditional festivals are held here in the second half of June, such as the "caragol," a medieval game on horseback.

The south coast of Minorca is rugged, and has a series of beautiful inlets, with dark green pine trees, sandy beaches, caves, and white cliffs eroded by the wind. Cala Santa Galdana is the most striking. It is spacious, almost round, and partially closed to the south by a mass of rocks. A stream runs down through the twisting valley and into the bay.

A stretch of sea twenty miles wide separates Minorca from its sister island of Majorca. One lands at Capdepera, at the northern tip of a high, rocky coast with Cape Vermell at its end. Immediately beyond this lies the beautiful bay of Cañamel, where the sea has scoured caves out of the rocks. The Caves of Artá have huge stalactites and the light and reflections have a magical effect. A few miles further south, near the natural harbour of Porto Cristo, are the famous Drach Caves, with four chambers of magnificent rock formations. Farther inland are the Hams caves with a network of interconnecting lakes which eventually join the sea.

The coast continues, full of bays, beaches, fishing villages and holiday resorts. Of particular interest are Cala Magraner, Cala Barqueta and Cala Virgili, reached through a broad cleft in the rocks; the little creek of Cala Arsenau, south of La Farola point, and

Cala Mitjana. Cala d'Or is a tourist resort with white sand, limpid water, rocks and pine trees, while Porto Petro is a fishing village set in a broad bay. Cala Figuera, in a cleft between high cliffs, is very attractive, despite some big modern hotels in the vicinity.

Beyond Cape Salinas at the southern tip of Majorca, the south-west coast is low to begin with, stretches of sand alternating with rocky beaches, and then develops into a monotonous line of off-white cliffs. Cala Pi is still completely wild, and is the last anchorage before the heavily built-up area of the bay of Palma.

Overleaf: a view of Cala Figuera, Majorca.

Below: Ciudadela is built at the end of a long, narrow inlet. Traces of its illustrious past as the capital of the island of Minorca are visible in the elegant mansions and picturesque vaults of the medieval quarter. This area is a maze of narrow streets, dominated by the Gothic cathedral.

RANEAN SEA

Odessa

R O M A N I A

Constanţa

adar

Split

BULGARIA

BLACK SEA

Dubrovnik

ADRIATIC SEA

Gargano

Bari

Istanbul

Taranto   Brindisi   Durrës   Thessaloniki   SEA OF MARMARA

C. S. Maria
di Leuca

C. Baba

Crotone

IONIAN SEA

Izmir

C. Spartivento

essina
atania
yracuse

Patraí   Peloponnisos   Athens

Bodrum   Antalya

Marmaris

Passero

Fethiye

C. Matapan   AEGEAN SEA   RHODES

C. Busa   CRETE   C. Sidheros   CYPRUS

Limassol

Benghazi   Tobruk

Port
Said

Sirte   Alexandria

E G Y P T

L I B Y A

Y U G O S L A V I A

A L B A N I A   G R E E C E

T U R K E Y

15°   20°   25°   30°